MW00678926

**Praise for**

*Extreme Marriage*

"Beyond writing one of the most engaging and helpful marriage books I've ever read, Terry Owens lives out the content in his own marriage. Treat yourself to this inspiring book!"

—BILL HYBELS, senior pastor, Willow Creek
Community Church

"A blood-pumping, pulse-racing book! Terry Owens goes beyond simply describing the rigors and rewards of marriage; he also equips couples to face the most exhilarating adventure of their lives. Full of vivid images and powerful insights, *Extreme Marriage* challenges spouses to strive for a higher level of energy, perseverance, and ultimate satisfaction in their relationship."

—JERAMY and JERUSHA CLARK, authors of *Define the
Relationship* and *I Gave Dating a Chance*

"*Extreme Marriage* is what every married or unmarried couple should read. It helps you understand daily struggles and opens your eyes to what is most important in a relationship."

—SETH KIMBROUGH, professional BMX rider
and singer with Mortal Treason

# extreme marriage

mastering the

ever-changing,

lifelong adventure

# TERRY OWENS

WATERBROOK
PRESS

EXTREME MARRIAGE
PUBLISHED BY WATERBROOK PRESS
2375 Telstar Drive, Suite 160
Colorado Springs, Colorado 80920
*A division of Random House, Inc.*

ISBN 1-57856-881-1

Library of Congress Cataloging-in-Publication Data
Owens, Terry, 1956-
  Extreme marriage : mastering the ever-changing, lifelong adventure / Terry Owens.— 1st ed.
      p. cm.
  Includes bibliographical references.
  ISBN 1-57856-881-1
  1. Spouses—Religious life. 2. Marriage—Religious aspects—Christianity.
3. Extreme sports—Miscellanea. I. Title.
  BV4596.M3O94 2004
  248.8'44—dc22

                        2004017406

Printed in the United States of America
2005

10  9  8  7  6  5  4  3  2

# contents

# Acknowledgments

This book is the result of an amazing process of people and circumstances coming together at just the right times. Simply thanking the following people doesn't do justice to the critical roles they have played. Without the unique and often indirect contributions each of them made to this project, you probably wouldn't be reading this right now. To acknowledge their contributions to this book is also to acknowledge the role each of us plays in the lives of others and the functioning of the church. It's a 1 Corinthians 12 thing.

Thank you, Hal, for encouraging Tari and me to get off the bench and into the game—and, Rick and JoAn, for giving us the chance. Finny, it was your response to those first thoughts that led me to believe I should get this thing going. Joe and Taylor, your support in my life and your encouragement on this project have been more significant than any of us can quantify. Mark, it was your insights that shed light on some dark areas of my heart and mind and enabled me to see the truth about the lies I believed. And once again, thank you, Finny, for staying in my face with the truth. Mike, I am grateful for your friendship and the example your life provides—challenged and humbled, but grateful. Jon, thank you for your friendship and for leading me to Jim. Jim, thank you for the introduction to Don.

Don, thank you for inviting me to join the WaterBrook team. Bruce, I can't imagine a better editor to work with. Jami, Mark, and

Carol, thank you for your efforts on my behalf. The work you do frees me to do what I love to do.

In Philippians 4:8, Paul encourages us to think about things that are excellent and praiseworthy. I am grateful to the extreme athletes I have written about. I do not know them personally, but their enthusiasm for and commitment to their sports have challenged me with clear examples of excellence. I have learned much about marriage from them and, as a result, am a better husband.

# Introduction

I t all started with *The Last River*, Todd Balf's account of a whitewater kayaking expedition on the Tsangpo River in Tibet. As I read about the awesome power of that river and the swirling, surging, rushing character of white water, I began to think that marriage was a lot like whitewater kayaking. As I reflected on adventure books I'd already read, like Jon Krakauer's *Into Thin Air* and Joe Simpson's *Touching the Void*, I kept coming back to the obvious applications to my marriage. At least they were obvious to me.

And when I read books like *The Seven Principles for Making Marriage Work* by John Gottman, *Boundaries in Marriage* by Henry Cloud and John Townsend, and *Sacred Sex* by Tim Alan Gardner, I wondered why everyone wasn't reading them. But everyone wasn't, even though the potential payoff was huge and obvious. And that troubled me, because marriage has enormous potential for either pervasive, soul-deep satisfaction or oppressive, crippling pain and disillusionment. You have to pursue satisfaction. Pain and disillusionment can just happen. And they often do.

I believe that every husband and wife want the kind of marriage that satisfies at the soul level, whether they recognize it or not. It's a kind of connection that many people don't even know is possible. But we don't have the necessary skills, or we don't know where to get them, or we aren't prepared to do the required work, either on ourselves or our marriage. And our fears pose a much bigger obstacle than we recognize or are willing to admit.

Which brings me to *Extreme Marriage.* It's at the confluence of two apparently different rivers: extreme sports and marriage. But on closer inspection, these two are a lot more alike than they are different. A passionate desire to succeed, a willingness to push to get better, a spirited sense of adventure, an incredible respect for nature (including the nature of their own hearts, minds, and bodies), a willingness to take risks—these are some of the things that characterize the extreme sport adventurer. They also characterize a person seeking a successful marriage.

In the big picture, I believe that if husbands and wives approached their marriages with the same enthusiasm and conviction that people in extreme sports approach their particular sports, our world would be a much better place. The difference would be dramatic and immediate. And as subsequent generations grew up in progressively healthier families, that improvement would continue. On a smaller but more personal scale, I know that if husbands and wives brought that same spirit to their relationship, their own worlds would be much better. This is the way life was supposed to be lived. The possibilities are too numerous to count.

I encourage you to explore them for yourself. You don't know what you'll find along the way. That's why it's an adventure.

Each chapter in *Extreme Marriage* explains an extreme sport and a specific marriage principle. Then it concludes with a short summary, which is followed by a couple of reflection questions to guide a couple's conversation. Also, a small-group discussion guide is available free of charge at www.waterbrookpress.com. Effective small groups can accelerate our development as spouses. With the help of others, each of us can become better faster. And who doesn't want to get better?

I hope and pray that this book is a catalyst for your growth. It's certainly been that for me.

# the most extreme of them all

## marriage is the ultimate challenge

> *Well, mates, this is a simple sport: do it right,*
> *you live—do it wrong, you don't.*
> STEVE WOODFORD, skydiving instructor

The most extreme of the extreme sports? What would you say it is?

Snowboarders might argue for their sport. The speeds at which they glide down a mountain and the balance required to stay upright certainly make it a demanding sport. High-altitude climbers would probably claim that the focus and determination necessary to ascend to the world's most extreme places, while battling the physically and mentally debilitating effects of altitude, make their sport the most extreme. Good point.

But triathletes could present a compelling case that the diverse proficiencies required to swim 2.4 miles, cycle 112 miles, and then wrap it all up with, oh, maybe a little 26.2-mile run, might make them the extremest of the extreme. Rock climbers might insist that the strength, balance, flexibility, and problem-solving resourceful-ness required to follow a crack that your fist couldn't fit sideways into, up a half mile of sheer stone face, pushing off footholds no big-ger than a teacup, make their sport worthy of the most extreme honor. And you could see their point, but cavers might suggest that the crawling, climbing, slithering, rappelling, and scuba-diving skills of spelunking put it, ironically, at the top of the extreme sports world. Add to those the fearlessness necessary to perform them, knowing that you are hundreds of feet below the earth's surface in a darkness that, except for the artificial light you brought with you, is so unimaginably black that your eyes would never adjust to it. It might be the most extreme.

Yeah, yeah, yeah. Speed, focus, determination, stamina, resource-fulness, fearlessness, whatever. Imagine what it would be like to do those things in *tandem*. You don't make a move without it somehow affecting your partner, and your partner doesn't make a move with-out it affecting you. What if the only way you can conclude your effort is with your teammate? No teammate, no finish. Hmmm, there's a different level of challenge.

Now imagine thirty years of falls, nicks, dings, spills, scrapes, and crashes, injuries too minor to worry about and others too big to ever completely forget. Imagine performing your sport better in thirty years than you do right now. The most extreme of the extreme sports is none of those mentioned above.

The most extreme of the extreme sports? It's the one most fre-quently attempted, but it also has the highest rate of failure. It's the one with the greatest number of uncontrollable variables and generally undertaken with the least amount of specific preparation. Not only does it have the highest incidence of failure, but it also has the most significant consequences for failure.

The most extreme of the extreme sports? Well, if you really want to see what you are made of, if you imagine yourself to be a risktaker, skilled, strong, resourceful, persevering, and able to perform complex tasks in a demanding environment, if you think you are up for the ultimate challenge—easily the most extreme of the extreme sports—try marriage. No, don't try marriage. Marriage is not something you try. It is something you do. And you either do it well or you don't.

Marriage, an extreme sport? Seriously?

Seriously! Whether you realize it or not, you're entering a river with a thundering Class V rapids downriver. Not to alarm you, but there will probably be a few, so you'd better know what you're doing. You're standing at the base of a rockface rated 5.13, what the British would call "extremely severe." Not difficult. Not severe or even very severe. *Extremely severe.* And if your heart's not pounding, you don't really know what you're getting into. You're entering a cave, at least you think it's a cave. It could be as life threatening as it is awe inspiring, and you don't have a map. There is no map. It's all new. This cave is unexplored, your skills untested.

That's a glimpse of the marriage adventure, a look ahead at the marriage challenge.

And if you don't think of marriage as a challenge, as an *extremely* extreme sport, why are so many people afraid of it? Maybe they intuitively understand what a huge commitment it is and how poorly prepared they are for it. Perhaps they know, at some level, what a huge risk it is to pledge yourself to someone, regardless of all the intervening variables, for a lifetime—and mean it.

Why are the emotional, psychological, and financial consequences of marriage so significant and pervasive in our country? Because all of us have a deep, never-satisfied need to know and to be known, to connect with others. And when our relationships, especially our marriages, disappoint us, we respond in anger and pain.

Extreme circumstances have a way of exposing the truth.

Why would anyone even try an activity with such consequences? Because, just like any extreme sport, we know that where the risk is great, so is the opportunity for reward. We could be badly hurt or, man, what a blast this could be. Intuitively, we know the awesome potential of marriage. And we also know how strong our natural desire is to be in relationship. Marriage is the ultimate risk/reward proving ground. It has as much upside potential as downside risk. There is such an opportunity for know-and-be-known companionship, and yet there is also no lonelier place than a failing marriage.

Extreme marriage is a redundant phrase. Marriage, properly understood, is extreme. There is simply no other way to look at it. What I'm talking about is not a marriage that begins with the hope that things will work out, whatever that means. And I'm not proposing a relationship resulting in some mild sense of happiness, a vague notion that things are okay. This is not a marriage that simply stays together till the kids are raised or looks good to people on the outside looking in.

What I have in mind is mastering a long-term, ever-changing, complex activity that has as much potential for extreme pain as it does enormous satisfaction. It will affect every area of your life and soul. It is the lifetime process of learning to love more effectively and completely the person you're marrying, the one you think you know, the one who is certain to change, maybe positively, maybe negatively, in response to challenges you can't even predict.

What's in it for you? The incredible rewards of intimate relationship! Generally, people on the outside of an extreme sport looking in don't understand the motivation or the exhilaration of those involved. They watch and wonder, *How do they do that? Why do they do that?* The same is true with a successful marriage. Often the outsiders looking in just don't grasp the sacrifice and skill required—or the tremendous satisfaction that comes from doing it right.

We're talking about extreme marriage. And if that is not your goal, then cop a squat, grab the remote and a bag of chips, and prepare to ooze into middle age. Unless you're planning on rising to the extreme challenge of having a great marriage, count on yours being a source of frustration, disappointment, pain, indifference, or maybe just a chronic sense that it should be more…something.

But marriage an extreme sport? Don't believe me? What makes an extreme sport extreme, anyway?

It's not necessarily the skill involved, though successful extreme athletes are skilled. Hitting a major-league fastball in baseball is one of the most difficult things to do in all of sports. But baseball is not an extreme sport. It's not necessarily about strength. NFL players spend countless hours in the weightroom getting bigger and stronger. And though professional football is certainly a demanding sport, it is not an extreme sport. How about speed, quickness, and stamina? An NBA iron man will run up and down the court an average of thirty-seven minutes a game. Of course, it's not just running. It's running, then stopping, then cutting, stopping and reversing, then jumping. It's doing all that on offense. It's doing all that on defense. It's doing all that against some of the world's most elite athletes over an eighty-two-game regular season schedule, plus another four rounds of playoff games if you're good enough. Extremely well-conditioned athletes play basketball, but it is not an extreme sport.

Skill, strength, speed, stamina—they are all characteristics of extreme sports but not the defining characteristics. So what makes an extreme sport extreme?

The first criterion is that you are competing in nature, not in a controlled setting like a stadium. No one has determined a formal standard for the field of competition, and no staff of groundskeepers is on the payroll to ensure it is safe and fair, clear of obstructions. Consequently, you are also competing against nature. Gravity, terrain, weather, and other external conditions are part of the team that opposes you, the team that you have to overcome in order to "win."

Another criterion is rules, or rather the absence of them. In most sports there are officials whose job it is to make sure the participants adhere to the rules determined by a rules committee. And if, in the course of the game, one of the officials observes a participant violating the rules, he will blow a whistle, throw a flag, or hold up a card and assess some form of penalty. Often a rules violation stops play.

In extreme sports there are no rule books administered on the field of play by nonparticipants, unless you're taking part in an organized competition. When you're doing extreme sports, there are judgments, not rules. If your judgments are correct and you execute them properly, you can succeed. If your judgments are incorrect or your execution's lacking, there are naturally occurring consequences.

Consequences are the third criterion of extreme sports. In football, an offensive lineman who crosses the line of scrimmage before a pass is thrown becomes an ineligible receiver, and his team is penalized. Basically, he has gone where he is not supposed to go. And though coaches will tell you that stupid mistakes will kill you, they don't really kill you. Not like a snowboarder, for instance, who could make a mistake, board right off the side of a mountain, and die. Now there's a consequence. Extreme sports involve danger.

And the final criterion of extreme sports, at least as they compare to the major sports—the ones with large television and stadium audiences—is that except for a zealous little subculture, no one really cares. If they did, Tanya Streeter would be a household name—she can hold her breath for six minutes under water. On July 21, 2003, she set a new free-diving world record by descending four hundred feet without any sort of breathing system, beating the previous record for women by eighty-eight feet and for men by six feet.

But free diving, like most extreme sports, doesn't receive a lot of attention in the mainstream media. It does illustrate the risk of extreme sports (another woman blacked out and died in pursuit of one of Tanya's records) as well as the need for good judgment.

You want to test your mettle against nature? Try the kind of nature that no structure, no piece of equipment or high-tech clothing can protect you from. It's inside-out nature. It's human nature, the desire all of us have to think first of ourselves.

"By nature, we are entirely *self-oriented,*" says Larry Crabb. This self-orientation shows up in our preference to have things our own way, to take what is, for us, the easy way out. Your marriage will be many things to you. But one thing it will not be is a refuge from this self-orientation. As a matter of fact, unless you admit that you are self-oriented, take the time to learn how you express your self-orientation, and most important, commit to ruthlessly battle it each day of your life, your marriage will likely become the place where your self-centeredness shows up most often.

"What marriage has done for me is hold up a mirror to my sin," admits Gary Thomas. "It forces me to face myself honestly and consider my character flaws, selfishness, and anti-Christian attitudes." Thomas isn't alone in suddenly becoming aware of his own shortcomings.

"Sometimes what is hard to take in the first years of marriage is not what we find out about our partner, but what we find out about ourselves," say Kathleen and Thomas Hart. "As one young woman who had been married about a year said, 'I always thought of myself as a patient and forgiving person. Then I began to wonder if that was just because I had never before gotten close to anyone. In marriage, when [we] began…dealing with our differences, I saw how small and unforgiving I could be. I discovered a hardness in me I had never experienced before.'"

The rules of the game? Well, there is no official rule book of marriage. No group of wise people have convened to agree on a formal set of rules for the marriage game to ensure fair play. No striped-shirt official is going to be assigned to oversee your marriage, ensuring your compliance with rules. You and your spouse will have to determine how best to apply biblical relationship guidelines to your marriage. The guidelines won't change, but the specifics of how you apply them over time will as you, your spouse, your family, and life circumstances change. And if the Bible is not the basis for the judgments you make, what is?

Television? Popular magazines? The relationship into which you were born or in which you grew up? Many influences have shaped the values you have. The values you have will determine the judgments you make. And the judgments you make will ultimately determine the quality of your marriage.

A failure in extreme sports may get you injured or killed. If you fail in marriage, parts of you and your spouse will be hurt and quite possibly will die. Your hope for the things that might have been, your confidence in your ability to be a good partner, your ability to trust and to give of yourself—all those things and more are badly damaged, perhaps fatally, in a failed marriage.

But the reverse is true as well. Get it right, and you can't imagine the possibilities. Your marriage will be a source of connectedness, motivation, confidence, and satisfaction. The bonding that occurs as two lives continue to grow together is an experience that many people, even many married people, never have.

But it's not just the two of you. It's your kids, and your kids' kids, and the kids of your kids' kids. Kids that will never have the chance to meet you will either benefit from your faithfulness to the challenge of extreme marriage, or they will suffer the consequences of your shortcomings.

Now those are some consequences.

And it all starts with you two. Whether you consciously accept the challenge or not, whether you get your marriage right or wrong, the choices you make and the kind of marriage you build will have a powerful effect on both of you and on generations of families to come. Will your heirs reap rewards or pay a price? If you get it right, no crowd is going to surround you, hoist you on their shoulders, and carry you triumphantly around the stadium. You won't get to smile at the camera and gush, "I'm going to Disneyland." Nike, Red Bull, and Columbia Sportswear will not be pestering your agent to lock up your endorsement.

As a matter of fact, as you set out on your marriage adventure with the hope for what yours can become and the determination to make it happen, don't be surprised if you get a little ridicule. Many people are uncomfortable seeing others succeed where they know they do not. Expect some people to roll their eyes. Expect some people to smirk and ask, "And how long have you been married?" as they wait for what they regard as the inevitable forces of time and life to bring you back to what they call "the real world."

God knew it was not good for people to be alone. We need to be in relationship. It's how He created us. And though all relationships are critically important, He knew that our best shot at the kind of community He had in mind was marriage, not because of the happiness it offers, but because of the growth it requires and the satisfaction it delivers. What He had in mind was extreme marriage, a purposefully, tirelessly, sacrificially loving relationship like Christ with the church.

Many people just don't know what's possible. They've never seen an extreme marriage and can't imagine the possibilities. They get hung up on the word *marriage*. When they hear *marriage*, they think dos and don'ts, obligations and restrictions. It's unfortunate, but predictable, that the same thing happens when many people hear the word *Christianity*.

"When you see 'Christianity' read, The Never-Ending Adventures and Journeys of the Jesus Followers," advises Don Everts in his book *Jesus with Dirty Feet*. Unfortunately, many people don't understand that following Jesus is supposed to be the adventure of a lifetime.

And the same is true of marriage. When we see the word *marriage*, we should read The Never-Ending Adventures and Journeys of the Jesus Followers in Life's Most Connected Companionship. It's an extreme idea. And it will stretch you to extremes. But it will also reward you to the extreme. And that's probably exactly what God had in mind, both for marriage and for you.

## SUMMARY

The desire for connection and companionship is a need that is hard-wired into our souls by the eternally relational God who created us. It's as strong in men as women, though how we express it and experience it may be different. Marriage offers us the greatest opportunity to satisfy that need, but it also creates the greatest potential for pain and disappointment. Get it right, and you can't imagine the possibilities. Get it wrong, and you can't imagine the consequences.

## FOR REFLECTION

1. What experiences and relationships have been most significant in preparing you for the marriage adventure?

2. Describe the biggest risk you've ever taken and the effect it had on you.

# The Greatest Race You Never Heard Of

## Agreeing on the Direction in Marriage Is Like an Adventure Race

> *The decision to become a Raid competitor was a turning point.... It marked a sea of change for me in ways I could not have foreseen. My life, and the way I viewed the world, would forever be altered, and in a most powerful and positive way.*
>
> MARTIN DUGARD, adventure racer

Y ou want to talk races? How about the hundred meters? It might be the perfect race.

What more could you ask for? It's got a dramatic start, an obvious finish, and all that pumping-arms, churning-legs action in between. And the best part? The whole thing, from the time the gun goes off to start it until the winner lunges across the finish line, takes less than ten seconds. No strategy. No boring interludes while runners jockey for position. Even a point-and-click, DSL society can pay attention for ten seconds.

A tidy little race. And a nifty title for the world recordholder: the World's Fastest Human.

There is another superlative in track and field: the World's Greatest Athlete. He's not the fastest or strongest. He cannot run the farthest nor jump the highest. He is never within a high hurdle of the world recordholders for the various individual events. The man with this lofty title is the winner of the decathlon, an event of events—ten different track-and-field skills performed individually for a combined score.

It is a demanding event. The diversity of skills required, the need to be at least proficient in all, and the physical conditioning necessary to perform them all over a two-day period make the winner of the Olympic decathlon worthy of the title World's Greatest Athlete.

The World's Fastest Human is one fast fellow, but fast is a pretty specialized skill, and a hundred-meter straightaway isn't exactly a navigational challenge. The World's Greatest Athlete is certainly great, but he knows exactly what events to prepare for, in what order they will be run, and that the stadium will be in the best possible condition. It's a solo effort, so the only performance he has to worry about is his own. And after two days, it's over. Wouldn't a few uncontrollable variables heighten the challenge considerably?

French journalist Gerard Fusil must have felt much the same way when he began to conceive of the Raid Gauloises, a race you've probably never heard of. It was the Eco-Challenge before there was an Eco-Challenge.

The Raid includes a wide variety of events done in a demanding, natural environment. It's kind of like the Ironman in Hawaii, first run in 1979, New Zealand's Coast to Coast, started in 1980, and the Alaska Wilderness Challenge, begun in 1983. Kind of like those, but not exactly.

What if the race environment changed every year, from the desert of Madagascar one year, to the jungles of Borneo the next, then on to high, windswept Patagonia the following year? That might make things a little more interesting.

And what if the individual events changed from year to year? Always a core group of events, including some combination of trekking, mountain biking, mountaineering, and some sort of paddling, but also location-specific challenges? Skydiving to begin the race in Madagascar, caving in Borneo's two-hundred-mile network of limestone caverns, ice climbing in Patagonia. The only certainty would be that whatever the events and their order were last year, they would be different next year, both of which would be different from the present year. That would keep things fresh.

And what if the course was long enough, maybe four hundred miles as it was in Patagonia, that the race would take days to complete, giving competitors the choice of racing through the night? Nothing like a little sleep deprivation to exacerbate fatigue and frustration.

Additionally, Fusil decided it was not good that man should

compete alone. What if the competition would be among teams, not individuals? What if you had to start as a five-person team, finish as a five-person team, and complete everything in between as a five-person team? That would bring a whole new level of challenge to the race.

Uncontrollable variables compounded by unknown circumstances over an undetermined period of time. Now that would be a test of character. That would be a race. There would be no World's Greatest Athlete, no World's Fastest Human. No superlatives of any kind. Just the title of Raid winner, the team that had whatever it took to cross the finish line first.

In 1989, after two years of development and securing corporate sponsorships, Fusil launched the first Raid in New Zealand, and the sport of adventure racing was born. Thirty-five teams started the race, a five-hundred-kilometer event that included treks through rain forests and up mountain peaks. Only six teams finished, the winner doing so in five days, twenty-one hours, and thirty-six minutes.

From 25 to 30 percent of an adventure race will be walking. Trekking would actually be a better word, because your little walk could take you through streams, over uneven talus and scree fields, and up muddy trails obstructed by the occasional downed tree. You could find yourself walking in sand (two times as hard as walking on grass or a paved surface), trudging through snow (three times as hard), or even bushwhacking (as much as five times slower in dense brush). You could find your joints and one set of muscles challenged by steep descents and a different set of muscles burning on the climbs.

Mountain biking is another of the core disciplines. Count on long uphill climbs and hike-a-bike sections in which rocks, logs, mud, or steep inclines require that you push your bike rather than ride. You could have multiple bike rides and cycle as much as ninety miles in a multiday adventure race. And don't be surprised if you have the opportunity to ride through the night. Many teams do.

About 25 percent of a normal adventure race, if there is such a thing, will be spent on water in canoes, kayaks, or rafts. The water can be as peaceful as a lake or as agitated as a section of Class III or IV white water. Because of river currents, it is possible to get farther faster with a more efficient use of energy than when trekking or mountain biking—if you know how to manage the currents. If you don't, river currents can flip your boat, exposing you to the discomfort of soaked clothes, potential hypothermia, wet food, and the dangers of getting banged into boulders or pinned in tree branches that have fallen in the river.

Mountaineering components are frequently part of adventure races. Such skills as rappelling, climbing on fixed ropes, and the Tyrolean traverse are examples. Some races might require that competitors know how to use an ice ax and crampons. Other races might include canyoneering, which will almost always involve rappelling down steep canyon walls or waterfalls and swimming or hiking in the streams at the bottom.

Adventure racers are always mindful of finishing, and that

means measuring and responding wisely to various challenges. It may be possible to bike up a steeply ascending, rock-strewn one-mile path, for example, but would it demand too much energy to effectively continue? You may lose time short term in order to maintain movement and, ultimately, to make better time. It's possible to win a battle and lose the war.

The recipe for adventure race challenges is always changing. Camel riding, skydiving, caving, in-line skating, hydrospeeding (whitewater swimming on a small raft or Boogie Board), and human-powered dogsledding are examples of disciplines that competitors have faced. The list is limited only by the imagination of the race organizers. Strengths and weaknesses being what they are, some racers will excel in some events and not others. But they have to be at least proficient enough to complete each part of the race.

Perhaps the most important skill in adventure racing is navigation. In a race in which the course can include unmarked jungles, confusing trail intersections, featureless plains, and night travel, the ability to know where you want to go, how you plan to get there, and what markers you look for along the way is critically important.

First of all, good navigation is efficient. A race that may take a week or more could be decided by an hour or less, so you can't afford to waste time. Second, in a race in which a single misjudged or careless step could result in an injury serious enough to end the race for you and, consequently, everyone else on your team, you can't afford the increased risk. Third, in a race in which many teams will drop out due to exhaustion, you can't afford to waste effort.

Discovering you've headed in the wrong direction is a huge physical hardship for any team, but the mental consequences may be worse. "More team disagreements, arguments and general team disintegration occur over issues related to navigation. The team's ability to recover after they discover that they went the wrong way will determine the success or failure of the team as a whole," say Liz Caldwell and Barry Siff, adventure racers and coauthors of *Adventure Racing: The Ultimate Guide.* The importance of knowing where you're going and where you are cannot be overemphasized. Neither can the potential for individual and team discouragement.

Just prior to the start of the race, competitors are given course maps. The entire course should be plotted when everyone is fresh and rested, and the whole team should be included. Trying to plot the course when you're shivering in the rain and haven't slept in twenty-four hours is a great way to make the kinds of mistakes that splinter a team and potentially end the race.

The course should be planned, but the team should be prepared to make adjustments as opportunities present themselves or challenges arise. It is, after all, an adventure race, not a hundred-meter dash.

Though one person on the team is primarily responsible for navigation, everyone should be involved. The lead navigator is as tired and uncomfortable as the rest of the team, so it helps when others know what rock formation to look for or when they should encounter a stream. It increases their likelihood of staying on course.

If navigation is the most important skill, then teammate selection is the most important decision.

In their book *Flow in Sports,* Mihaly Csikszentmihalyi and Susan Jackson point out that our word *competition* comes from the two Latin words *con petire,* which literally mean "to search together." The idea was that being paired against another would draw out our best efforts. Forget winning or demonstrating superiority over someone else. By searching together, we would become better than we could be if we searched alone. Who you search with in an adventure race is critical.

"Everyone's personality will be amplified during a race," say Caldwell and Siff. That's important to know when you could find yourself five days into the race, going without sleep for the last twenty-four hours, walking on already blistered feet, hurrying to make up for the hour you lost after taking the wrong trail, and trying to get to the water section before the cutoff time so that you and your sore back can paddle for another hour or two.

As any Raid progresses, so do fatigue, discomfort, and the monotony of so much effort for so little apparent progress. And as fatigue, discomfort, and monotony build, well…everyone's personality will be amplified. Will you quit the race or continue? Will you be a people builder who contributes positively to the team or someone who complains about everything from your teammates to the weather? Are you flexible enough to solve unforeseen problems and take advantage of unexpected opportunities, or does change paralyze you?

Extreme sports can lay bare your soul, in case you want to know what's in there. Extreme sports in a team setting can lay bare your soul for others to see. It's as true in marriage as any other extreme sport.

## THE GOAL OF YOUR MARRIAGE ADVENTURE

If navigation is critical to the success of an adventure racing team, how much more critical is it to a marriage team? Where are you going in your marriage? What do you want to accomplish? What do you want your marriage to be about?

"What if God designed marriage to make us holy more than to make us happy?" asks Gary Thomas. What if our success or failure in marriage was measured primarily by whether or not we were becoming more and more like Christ in the way we related to our husband or wife? What if we lived as though marriage was the most important tool in our development into more complete Christ followers? What other goals might there be? If you looked at someone's marriage and said, "That is a successful marriage," what characteristics would you be seeing?

Does staying married and not getting a divorce mean your marriage is a success? How about staying sexually faithful? Probably not. We've all seen couples go through the motions of staying together and apparently remaining faithful but who live as roommates. The resulting loneliness, fear, indifference, and even hardheartedness for both husband and wife make them progressively less like Jesus, not more. Staying married and sexually faithful are critical and necessary components, but they are not the goal.

How about the number of arguments you have, the way your marriage looks to those on the outside, the success you have in business, the address at which you live, the kinds of cars you drive, the kids you raise, and the schools they attend? Does any one or combination of those strike you as an accurate measure for the success of your marriage? To some extent we should be concerned about all of those things, but are they the standard by which you want your marriage relationship to be judged?

Does it seem odd to you that in a country so consumed with measures of success, we don't talk much about what qualifies as a successful marriage?

How about happiness? Maybe you thought God intended for marriage to make us happy. Make your spouse happy. Make your kids happy. And after everyone else of course, make you happy. As long as you're all happy, what else is there?

"The worst value ever," is how John Townsend and Henry Cloud describe happiness. "The reason is that happiness is a result. It is sometimes the result of having good things happen. But usually it is the result of our being in a good place inside ourselves and our having done the character work we need to do so that we are content and joyful in whatever circumstance we find ourselves. Happiness is a fruit of a lot of hard work in relationships, career, spiritual growth, or a host of other arenas of life. But nowhere is this as true as in marriage."

You will experience many things in marriage; one of them is bound to be happiness. But it can't and shouldn't be a goal. When you chase happiness, you tend to pursue either your own pleasure or the approval of others.

On the other hand, unhappiness is not a goal either. But it will be a part of your marriage, at least once in a while. Maybe for a long while. And maybe you will never be happy with some aspect of your spouse. Even a great marriage is not always happy. Watch out. Unhappy people tend to look for the cause of their unhappiness and often decide that it is their job, their home, their spouse. Whatever the cause, most often it is "out there," some external circumstance that stands between them and happiness. If only they had a better-paying job, a nicer house, a more sexually responsive wife, or a more emotionally attentive husband, then they would be happy.

Or they may blame themselves for either their own unhappiness or their spouse's. If only they were different or successful, less of one thing and more of another, happiness would inevitably result. But someone is unhappy, so it must be their fault.

For many people, happiness is associated with good things, unhappiness with bad. But short-term happiness may conflict with long-term benefit. Just because there is discomfort or it feels as though something bad is happening, that doesn't mean there isn't benefit. The happiness Cloud and Townsend are talking about is more than just a good feeling under the right circumstances. It is more like the satisfaction that comes from knowing you are doing a difficult thing well.

## What God Might Have Had in Mind

"God's ultimate goal for your life on earth is not comfort, but character development," says Rick Warren in his book *The Purpose-Driven Life.* "He wants you to grow up spiritually and become like Christ." Maybe it's what God had in mind when he said, "It's not good that man should be alone." If you're serious about character development and growing up spiritually, you have picked the perfect environment in marriage. But if you're more concerned about happiness, the approval of others, or lifestyle, expect problems.

"If you want to become more like Jesus," suggests Gary Thomas, "I can't imagine a better thing to do than to get married. Being married forces you to face some character issues you'd never have to face otherwise."

My wife, Tari, and I have a successful relationship, though we both admit we have plenty of room for additional growth. And if becoming more like Jesus is our ultimate goal, there always will be room for growth. Though our marriage meets those common, vague standards of a "good marriage," that's not why I'd call it successful.

One reason I'd call it successful is that we continue the never-ending process of developing our relationship with each other. Sometimes because of what we know and find out about each other, and sometimes in spite of it. We never assume our relationship will just take care of itself.

Another reason I'd call it successful is that we are becoming increasingly free of anger, dissension, selfishness, and worldly desires, the acts of our own particular sinful natures, that Paul lists in Galatians 5:19–21. And we are growing in the love, joy, peace, self-control, and other fruit of the Spirit promised by Paul in verses 22 and 23. It's a developmental process that, unfortunately, can't be short-cut. And it's a process that's catalyzed by our marriage.

"The good news is, you get to help each other grow," Tari often says. "The bad news is, you get to help each other grow." Much like a Raid team, we've learned to lean on each other, even in our imperfections, even when we're both tired, even when we've both wondered of each other, *Why can't you just   (fill in the blank)   so my life would be easier?* The grace that Christ extended to us, we now get to extend to each other as we assist one another on our race toward acquiring Jesus's character. Our companionship deepens, and our sense of team is strengthened in the process.

It can be easy to create the appearance of Christlikeness outside of marriage. But the daily best-of-times/worst-of-times, two-have-become-one quality of marriage makes it unique from our work relationships, our friendships and social acquaintances, our ministry involvements, or even other family relationships. In marriage you can run, and people do, but you can't hide, though people try. Christlikeness is not an appearance judged from the outside looking in. It is an attitude lived from the inside out. You are who you are, and for better or worse, who you really are will be revealed in the marriage adventure.

The sooner you decide what success in marriage looks like to you, the better off you'll be. Experienced navigators know that if you start out only one degree off at your point of departure, you can quickly get dangerously off course. The longer you're off course, the farther off course you'll go, and the more effort will be required to correct your situation, at a time when you may feel like you have nothing left to give. That's when many people get discouraged and quit.

You need to know where you're going. And regardless of whatever other worthy things you are pursuing, above all else, you need to be pursuing the character of Christ for yourself.

## COMMUNICATION WITHIN THE TEAM

A marriage team should be as communicative as a Raid team. Always knowing what becoming more like Jesus means to them. Always knowing where they are on the map. Always moving toward the goal. Always knowing what each other's challenges and satisfactions are. Always helping each other out. Always encouraging one another and maintaining a constant dialogue to make sure everyone is involved and the team is on track. In a hectic life it is easy to get distracted, lose sight of the goal, and substitute busyness for purposefulness, happiness or pleasure for satisfaction.

The roles you play in marriage are numerous, interrelated, and dynamic. A partial list includes friend, lover, financial partner, partner in parenthood if you choose to have children, caregiver, and partner in daily life maintenance. Some roles you will naturally do better than others, but excellence in one area is not an excuse to ignore the others. For practical life-maintenance matters, you will probably develop a relationship division of labor for each of you to do the things you do well and not to do the things you don't do well. But when it comes to relationship skills, you need to be base-level competent in all areas. You also need to be willing to learn and grow, because you don't know what will be required of you, when it will be required, or for how long.

The expectations you and your spouse have of each other will ebb and flow as life progresses. And life will progress, through your twenties, thirties, forties, fifties, sixties—who knows how long? Through twenty years of marriage? Maybe thirty? Forty possibly? How about fifty?

Uncontrollable variables compounded by unknown circumstances over an undetermined period of time. Marriage will lay bare your soul, in case you want to know what's in there. Not everyone does. Extreme marriage reveals your soul for your spouse to see, something that many people want even less. Just remember, it is not a ten-second sprint, a controlled two-day event of events, or even a six-day adventure race. It is a lifetime adventure.

## SUMMARY

Marriage is an adventure race. Becoming more like Jesus is the overarching goal, the finish line you never reach. Some of the sections include parenting, careers, and other relationships. There are many others, too numerous to mention. As a team, you must compete in each section. As individuals, each of you is responsible for preserving and building team harmony and spirit.

## FOR REFLECTION

1. Not counting love and compassion, the easy to identify and potentially vague traits, what are examples of specific characteristics you see in Jesus that you think will be especially helpful in your marriage?

2. Discuss two examples of situations in your life that, because of unexpected developments or unforeseen circumstances, required you to adapt.

## You Don't Just Show Up and Go Up—
## A Step Back for Couples Still Dating

### Getting to Know Someone Is Like Acclimatizing
### for a High-Altitude Climb

*Generally speaking, the slower the climb,*
*the better will be the acclimatization.*

DR. CHARLES HOUSTON, specialist in the effects of altitude on the body

aken abruptly from sea level to the summit of Mount Everest, an unacclimatized person would have only five to ten minutes of decreasing consciousness before lapsing into a coma and dying in about thirty minutes." So, in about the time it takes to watch a rerun of *Friends,* you could be dead simply because your environment changed dramatically in ways you weren't prepared for.

Mount Everest is the highest place on earth at 29,035 feet. And if you climbed Everest you would quickly notice how different it is from the place you call home. You'd notice how cold it is, how dry it is, how windy it is, how bright it is, how void of life it is. But the difference you will be most acutely aware of is how hard it is to breathe in such thin air.

"At sea level, a normal person at an exhaustive level of exercise spends only 7% of his energy breathing," says Dr. Robert Schoene, a specialist in the body and altitude's effect on it. "On the summit of Everest, about 30% of a climber's oxygen intake goes to the physical act of breathing."

Breathing—you've been doing it while you've been reading this book but probably haven't thought once about it. An average person will breathe 12 to 20 times per minute. So if we take 16 as the midpoint, that's about 960 breaths in a normal hour, or about 23,000 breaths a day. Good thing you don't have to think about it.

When you breathe, you expand your chest, creating lower pressure, a condition that is corrected by air rushing into your lungs. The air is cleaned, warmed, and moistened on its way to the approximately three hundred million little air sacs called alveoli. The alveoli take oxygen and diffuse it into the capillaries that surround your lungs. Those capillaries feed this newly oxygenated blood into a network of progressively larger veins for its return trip to the heart. The heart takes its cut of the oxygen and pumps the blood back out into the rest of your body via a progressively smaller system of arteries, veins, and capillaries. The capillaries deliver their cargo of oxygen to the blood and to individual cells.

You wouldn't have been able to comp out of a biology course with that explanation, but that's pretty much how it works. And it works because at sea level the air pressure is a stable 14.7 pounds per square inch. It is an environment we are entirely adapted to. Your body, a tremendously complex, dynamic network of interrelated systems, is set for it.

As you ascend, however, the air pressure decreases. At nine thousand feet, air pressure is about 75 percent of what it is at sea level; at eighteen thousand feet, 50 percent. On the summit of Everest, air pressure is about 30 percent of sea-level pressure. Consequently, each breath you take delivers less oxygen to your lungs.

So let's say you take a quick trip to nine thousand feet, the lower end of the range known as high altitude. It's possible you would soon find yourself experiencing some combination of a headache, malaise, loss of appetite, nausea, vomiting, edema (a retention of fluid often resulting in swelling), disturbed sleep, cyanosis (a condition marked by a bluish appearance in the fingernail beds, in the mucous membranes, and around the mouth), and ataxia (a difficulty in maintaining balance).

These symptoms indicate a condition called acute mountain sickness, or AMS. You probably shouldn't worry. Generally, in three to four days, if you drink a lot of water and limit your activity, your body will make the base-level adjustments necessary to begin the more significant adjustments required to ascend to the summit.

These adjustments, or acclimatization, are a group of physical adaptations your body makes in order to deal with the new oxygen-deficient environment. Without becoming acclimatized to life at altitude, no amount of equipment or climbing technique will keep you alive on your summit attempt.

The rate of ascent is the most important determinant of whether an individual develops mountain sickness. The general formula for acclimatizing to altitude is to ascend two thousand to three thousand feet each day and then come back down one thousand or so to sleep. Climb high and sleep low. And for every three thousand feet gained, take an extra day to rest.

In time, with specific and purposeful activity, your body adapts to the environmental changes. How much time? That depends on a lot of things. From what altitude did you come? How high are you going? What kind of shape are you already in? And a host of other physical predispositions you can't control.

Your body makes some immediate adjustments. You breathe faster and deeper, trying to get more oxygen deep into your lungs. Your heart beats faster, trying to compensate for the lower concentration of oxygen in the blood by increasing the amount of blood. And there are fluid shifts, like the brain receiving more blood, for example.

Your heart pumps more blood to the brain. More blood to the brain means the cerebral system is taxed and you'll get a headache.

In two to six days you'll grow accustomed to the increased blood flow, and the headaches will subside. Your rate of breathing will peak in about seven days, then start to decrease slowly. Your heart rate should begin returning to a more normal range in about ten days. In general, about 80 percent of the adaptations you will make are done in the first ten days or so.

In addition to the early adaptations, your body begins a series of changes that take a little longer, like stepping up production of oxygen-carrying red blood cells and substances in the blood that improve its ability to carry oxygen. Eventually, the number of capillaries, those circulatory foot soldiers that diffuse new oxygen into the blood and deliver the oxygen to individual cells, also increases. By six weeks you will be 95 percent acclimatized. That doesn't mean you function at 95 percent of your sea-level best when you are at altitude. It means that after six weeks, you probably aren't going to get any more adapted.

And you don't have to think about any of this. Whether you consciously choose to or not, your brain assesses the changes in the environment, their effects on your body, and makes the necessary adjustments.

Ah, the brain, the organ that is most vulnerable to environmental changes but also most critical in interpreting, both consciously and subconsciously, the information about this new environment. Your brain accounts for about 2 percent of your body weight but consumes up to 15 percent of the body's oxygen. Normally your blood unloads a rich payload of oxygen to your brain cells. Consequently, you perceive things with great insight, draw brilliant conclusions, and execute decisions flawlessly. But that's at sea level.

You simply don't think as well or as quickly at altitude. Stay at extreme altitude for any length of time and you may start to converse with people who aren't there, hear orchestras that aren't playing, or believe you can fly. That sounds funny, unless your diminished mental abilities cause you to make a fatal mistake, like walk off the side of the mountain or decide that twenty-eight thousand feet is a great place to take a little nap.

Experienced climbers know that two things are likely to happen as they near the summit. Even after acclimatization, they will continue to experience the effects of altitude. Above seventeen thousand feet or so, your body never fully acclimatizes. Above twenty thousand feet, it begins to deteriorate.

Decision making also begins to deteriorate. Climbers near the summit can't be counted on to think clearly or make wise decisions. Their judgment, already impaired, will become even more so. They can get caught up in emotion. They have trained for the climb. They have made financial and personal sacrifices to be on the trip. They have worked for the summit. They have spent weeks acclimatizing to progressively higher altitudes. The fact that they even chose climbing suggests that they are unusually purposeful, maybe even stubborn people who are accustomed to overcoming obstacles that stand between them and their goals. It's a situation in which the momentum of the endeavor can overcome good judgment.

Experienced climbers establish decision-making criteria before there are decisions to be made. They do so when they are still relatively clearheaded and not caught up in the emotion of the summit attempt.

They set a turnaround time. It's an objective standard by which they can say, "This is not going to work. Regardless of where I am on the mountain, how far I have come, and what I have invested in this endeavor physically, emotionally, and financially, I know if I don't abandon this summit attempt I could quite possibly die."

Experienced climbers also know what to look for in assessing a mountain's danger. They know that summiting Everest is a great accomplishment. Not so great if you don't get back down.

No American is better qualified to address high-altitude decision making than Ed Viesturs. On his first attempt of Everest in 1987, he and climbing partner, Eric Simonson, got to within three hundred feet of the summit. They knew they could reach it but also knew they couldn't safely descend. So after all the work and time they had invested, they abandoned the climb. Viesturs attempted Everest again in 1988 via the East Face. Once again he found the conditions unacceptable for a summit attempt.

"I realized that the attempt was not in line with my climbing philosophy.... The face was blatantly dangerous," he remembers. The third time was a charm in 1990 when Viesturs finally made it to the top of the world.

It almost seems that Viesturs turns back as often as he succeeds. In 1993 he turned back only twenty vertical feet from the summit of Shishapangma. In 1995 he and the late Rob Hall turned back the team they were guiding only three hundred feet short of Everest's peak. In 1998 he turned back on Dhaulagiri. He turned back on Nanga Parbat in 2001. Annapurna has bested him twice, once in 2000 and again in 2002.

A record of futility? Hardly. It's a testimony to wise decision making.

"Climbing a mountain has to be a round trip," says Viesturs. He should know. The Himalayas are home to fourteen eight-thousand-meter peaks. He is the only American to have summited thirteen of them.

"Getting up is optional," he says. "Getting down is mandatory."

## RELATIONAL ACCLIMATIZATION

Marriage is not a great accomplishment. People do it all the time. A *successful* marriage is a great accomplishment. Marriage is the summit of relationships because two people become one. Before attempting the marriage summit, however, you'll need to acclimatize.

Being single is much like living at relational sea level. You make a lot of decisions—where you go, how you act, what you do, who you do things with, what you think about, how you spend your time and money—based primarily on how you are going to be affected. And though you may be a wonderful person, generous to the point of sacrifice, considerate enough to embarrass an eagle scout, your decisions primarily affect you. Marriage is a much different environment, even from a serious dating relationship.

When two become one, the decisions you make also affect your spouse. Your chief focus in life is no longer yourself. Your chief focus is the well-being of your spouse. Not her happiness, not his approval, but the other's well-being. And if becoming more like Christ is your goal, then you should be building a relational environment that contributes to both of you becoming more like Jesus.

In acclimatization, your body understands that the environment is different and makes the necessary adjustments because it knows it will be very painful or even fatal if it doesn't. Unfortunately, the adaptations required to ascend the summit of marriage are not automatic. What is automatic is the way we cling to our self-centeredness, our preference for having things our way.

Relational acclimatization is a choice, a daily choice, a series of daily choices to think first of your spouse-to-be and to act in his or her best interest and in ways that benefit your relationship. What affects you, positively or negatively, also affects your loved one.

## Learn About Yourself

The first step in this marriage acclimatization process should have begun long ago. Let's call it purposeful self-knowledge. You learn about yourself, your strengths and your weaknesses, what you like and what you don't like. Learning how you express your self-orientation is critical because it will come up again and again and again in your marriage. If you are dating with the idea of finding a lifetime companion, the more you know about yourself, the easier the search.

"Dating efficiency is a function of clear thinking; you become more and more 'dating proficient' as you learn to think clearly about yourself and the person you want to marry," says Neil Clark Warren in *How to Know If Someone Is Worth Pursuing in Two Dates or Less.* Think clearly about ourselves? That's not something we're necessarily trained to do. We spend so much time around ourselves that one would think we'd know all about ourselves and be able to clearly state our needs, expectations, and desires. That's not necessarily true, even though there's abundant data. You just haven't been trained how to observe what's going on or systematically assemble what you do see.

How do you learn to think clearly about yourself? You ask yourself questions and make yourself answer, the same thing you would do if you wanted to get to know someone else.

Who are the most significant people in your life, both positive and negative? What is it about them that attracts or annoys you? What activities do you find yourself giving your best efforts to? What ideas do you find yourself often thinking about? What do you do in your spare time? What things do you like and not like about your work? How do you approach daily life-management issues—time, money, work, your physical environment, and your physical appearance?

What were the relationships like in your family? How did you relate to your parents and your parents to you? How about you and your siblings?

The work people have done in the process of self-discovery is a good indicator of their relationship work ethic. How well do they know themselves? Have they done the work necessary to know what kind of spouse they need and what kind of spouse they'd be? If they have not done the work on themselves, it will be a challenge to work on a relationship.

"The payoff for all this self-discovery and self-awareness is simple but profound: Men and women who know themselves well stand an excellent chance of selecting a mate well suited to them," says Warren. If you're honest and faithful to the process, a clearer picture of who you are will begin to emerge. And as this picture emerges, take that knowledge a step further and assemble a list of what Warren calls Must-Haves, qualities your ideal mate must have, and Can't-Stands, characteristics that kill the deal. Those become the things you look for in your dating relationships.

The further we go in relationship, the stronger the emotional bonds often grow, and the more difficult it can be to think clearly or to act on the clear thoughts you do have. It's important to have decision-making criteria set up before the decision has a face to go with it and relationship momentum behind it. Selecting a lifetime partner is a huge decision. The key to making a wise big decision— "This is the one I choose to marry"—is to make wise incremental decisions along the way.

## LEARN ABOUT YOUR DATING COMPANION

When you have asked those questions of yourself and have developed an accurate picture, you can do it honestly and respectfully with dates. Be as purposeful in learning about others as you are in learning about yourself.

You ask questions, questions that are related to the things you want to find out, and you listen for answers. You're not judging the person. It's not a matter of your being good enough for that person or that person being good enough for you. You are determining the potential for the person to be a good fit for a lifetime with you.

You are setting relationship precedents when you are dating. You are creating a pattern of relating to each other. Take the time to develop solid relationship skills and techniques. The dailiness of marriage reinforces our relationship habits, regardless of whether they are helpful to the marriage or hurtful. Patterns grow increasingly strong over time. So we have to make wise choices initially about how we are going to relate to each other.

Continue the relationship or don't continue the relationship. But either way, know why. Develop your decision-making criteria and stick to them. If you determine a person possesses those qualities, then continue the process of discovery over an extended period of time. Be purposeful. A dating relationship that drifts is setting a precedent for a marriage that drifts.

An enormous amount of research has been devoted to identifying and analyzing people's temperaments and personalities. If we believe in a God who creates, and we think He wasn't kidding when one of His inspired messengers wrote "For you created my inmost being; you knit me together in my mother's womb. I praise you because I am fearfully and wonderfully made," maybe we should do some follow-up research on our own. We can learn a lot about ourselves by taking a personality or temperament test. Four hundred years before Christ, Hippocrates attempted to explain the differences he noted in people by assigning them to one of four groups. In *Personality Plus,* Florence Littauer adds modern-day descriptors to update our understanding. Someone who is a Popular Sanguine is characterized as an extrovert, a talker, and an optimist. The Perfect Melancholy is described as an introvert, a thinker, and a pessimist. A person who tests as a Powerful Choleric tends to be an extrovert, a doer, and an optimist. And someone who tests as a Peaceful Phlegmatic is most likely an introvert, a watcher, and a pessimist.

Gary Smalley and John Trent simplify the personality variables by using animal descriptors. Lions (Cholerics) are characterized by strength and dominance, Otters (Sanguines) by their engaging playfulness. Beavers (Melancholies) are recognized by their industriousness and desire for perfection, and Golden Retrievers (Phlegmatics) by their steadfast loyalty. Business literature will often use the less playful descriptors of Driver (Choleric/Lion), Expressive (Sanguine/Otter), Analytical (Melancholy/Beaver), and Amiable (Phlegmatic/Golden Retriever).

The point is not what test we take or what descriptors we use. The point is that we were created to be different. No personality is right and no personality is wrong, though some may be better suited to specific circumstances than others. All have their own potential strengths and weaknesses. As a matter of fact, Smalley and Trent conclude: "Almost without exception, our weaknesses are simply a reflection of our strengths being pushed too far."

We are all different, and it often seems either tragic or comical that we are drawn to a mate who is different from us. For instance, Popular Sanguines often marry Perfect Melancholies. But problems arise when they tire of feeling like they have to energize and cheer up their more serious mates. They also grow weary of feeling inadequate or stupid compared to the analytical, intellectual Melancholies. Peaceful Phlegmatics tend to marry Powerful Cholerics but can grow to resent feeling pushed around and looked down upon.

Tari and I are great examples of this. For all the core values we share, you cannot imagine two people who are more consistently different from each other. Tari tests primarily as a Popular Sanguine with additional characteristics of a Powerful Choleric. My dominant characteristics are those of a Peaceful Phlegmatic, followed by traits associated with a Perfect Melancholy.

Intellectually, we knew about our differences. We dated for nine years. Long story. We'd taken the tests and knew we could expect challenges. And yet both of us admit we've spent way too much time and emotional energy either trying to change each other or waiting for the other to change. We now do a much better job of honoring each other's differences, but it's still something we have to work on, especially when we share new experiences or face conflict. Differences do attract and our strengths become our weaknesses, and all could contribute to challenging marriages.

Of course, it could also be a brilliant design that we tend to seek out people who are strong where we are weak and weak where we are strong. We usually don't choose people who are off-the-charts different or whose core values we don't share; instead, we choose those who are different enough that there is no shortage of opportunities for mutual growth and understanding. And perhaps, when two different people become one, together they form a more complete representation of the God who created them both.

It's these differences that often initially attract us to our spouse. But often what was attractive and endearing can one day become divisive and annoying. Unless you have an understanding of the dynamics of temperament and commit to understand and embrace those differences as part of your relationship, you will always struggle with acceptance of each other. Your harmony and respect for each other will be undermined, and you will waste a ton of emotional energy trying to either pound or manipulate your partner or yourself into something either of you is not.

You should be concerned not only with who you are and who your partner is but also with who you are when you are with each other.

## LEARN ABOUT YOURSELF AND EACH OTHER

Once you think you have learned about yourself and determined that another person has the qualities you are looking for, take the time to observe behavior, yours and your partner's. Acclimatize to being in relationship with this person. You may believe he or she is a person with whom you could make marriage work, but is that really the case? Behavior is a great indicator of what a person really believes.

When observing behavior, look for consistency between words and actions over a long period of time. Inconsistency takes awhile to show up. Or maybe it is just our ability or willingness to see it that takes awhile. Where there is no consistency between words and actions, there are gaps. Deception and isolation will fill those gaps. Eventually those will be the death of your ability to relate authentically with a person and to have a successful extreme marriage.

"If you and your partner do not have the freedom to be fully and authentically yourselves, the relationship is sure to remain unfulfilling," says Warren. Part of the dating process involves developing the trust to progressively reveal more of ourselves. That takes time. Remember, you're not racing up the mountain.

Another reason to take your time in dating is that you are trying to learn what your mate's needs are and how to meet them. This process isn't all about finding someone who you think can meet your needs and expectations. That is part of it, but it is just as important that you understand what his or her needs are and whether or not you are up for the challenge of meeting them, because it will be a challenge. You are looking for a good fit for yourself, and you are looking to be a good fit for someone else.

You can improve the efficiency at which your body performs at high altitudes, but you will only adapt so far. People do ascend to the summit of Everest, but the highest elevation of permanent human habitation is 16,730 feet, at La Rinconada in Peru. And at about 25,000 feet, you are in the appropriately named Death Zone, a place where you will die due to lack of oxygen and related effects.

Likewise, we can all learn to be more focused on the needs and well-being of our spouse, but we cannot live an entirely selfless life.

Yes, we are self-oriented, but we also have legitimate needs, expectations, and desires. It's possible for two people to date and never learn to balance both sets of interests at the same time. In the throes of a love that is not fully developed, regardless of how strong that love is, it can be a challenge to balance giving and receiving. Some people are strong in giving but fall short in receiving. Others are great at expressing their own needs but not so great at meeting the needs of others.

You want to make an informed choice in dating, because in marriage you get the person as a whole package, the good and the bad. And all of us have both. You can't pick and choose your mate's character qualities, accepting some and rejecting others. You either accept the person as he or she is or you don't. You may participate in your mate's growth, but your acceptance of the person needs to be complete and unconditional.

Ed Viesturs is preparing for his fourteenth eight-thousand-meter peak. Though he is a climbing legend, he still has to acclimatize for each climb. His body needs the time. He has the skill and perseverance necessary to make the climbs, but he also knows when to press on and when to turn back. He knows what avalanche conditions look like. He knows how weather affects climbing conditions. And he knows himself and his climbing partner, what they are capable of and what they are not.

You can do the hard work of self-discovery on your own and in your dating relationships. You can also be purposeful about searching for someone who is as good a fit for you as you are for him or her. And you can take your time to do both right. But you don't have to. There is an alternative. If you don't feel like doing the hard work before you say, "I do," you will do the potentially painful work of discovery within your marriage. Needs, expectations, and desires—yours and your spouse's—have a funny way of becoming remarkably clear when they are not met. You may have once been blind, but you will eventually see.

## SUMMARY

By learning about your likes and dislikes, your strengths and weaknesses, and your relationship tendencies, you gain a better understanding of yourself. By first dating, then marrying, with those in mind, you improve your chances of finding a spouse with whom you can build a mutually satisfying, lifelong marriage. But regardless of how well you know yourself and how well matched you are to your partner, expect that you will still have to work at making your marriage all it can be.

## FOR REFLECTION

1.  Based on what you know about your strengths and weaknesses, what characteristics would your ideal mate have?
2.  Based on what you know about yourself and your potential mate, where do you anticipate there will be friction in your relationship?

# up a wall without a piton

## overcoming a sense of entitlement in marriage is like rock climbing

> *You don't know if you can get there,*
> *you don't know what's going to happen to you*
> *before you really, actually try, and that was*
> *the way with El Cap. It was just a big unknown.*
>
> ROYAL ROBBINS, pioneer big wall climber

It was a life-changing encounter at the top of El Capitan. Life-changing? Sure, the phrase is overused, but this one really was. El Cap appears to erupt from the Yosemite meadow to a flat top three thousand feet in the air. Its sheer walls are hard, smooth granite. It is regarded with reverential awe by those in the rock-climbing community. Yes, there are taller faces and climbs where the weather is not nearly as accommodating as Southern California's, but the purity and magnificence of El Cap is unsurpassed. It is the quintessential big wall.

A big wall is loosely defined as a huge rock, at least vertical in angle, usually requiring several days to ascend. You might want to stop and think about that last part, the "several days to ascend" part. Several days means the climb will be measured in thousands of feet, not hundreds. Several days means that in addition to themselves, a climber and his partner have to get a hundred-pound (or more) haul bag of supplies up the face. Several days also means several nights, as in sleeping a couple of thousand feet off the ground on either a natural ledge, if one can be found, or on a "porta-ledge," a three-by-seven-foot platform of hollow aluminum tubes and nylon fabric.

Several days means that unless you are consumed by a passion to get to the top, stay on the ground.

Daniel Duane had been consumed by a need to climb El Cap since his early twenties. He attempted the climb three times in the summer of 1991, his fourth year of climbing. All three attempts failed, the first coming on a traverse halfway through the first day.

"The exposure…preyed upon the stability of my mind. My thoughts began to swirl about uncontrollably and I felt a terrible, inchoate urgency, as if something absolutely had to be done, and very, very soon." So he did something. He yielded to fear and descended.

His second attempt of the summer lasted into the third day, about two thousand feet up the wall. The end came when he dropped a bag of rain gear and warm clothing. Maybe it unnerved him to watch something silently fall two thousand feet before crashing into the ground below. Deciding he could go no farther, he and his partner rappelled down.

The third time was no charm. "I was utterly and desperately terrified once again. I actually wept with fear." Then came the summer of 1992 when he returned with the two climbing partners who had accompanied him on his failed attempts.

"The single greatest adventure of my life," is how Duane described his five and a half days on the Salathé Wall. "Sleeping on small ledges high in space, dangling on ropes from overhanging headwalls, and living day after day inside the security of total purpose.... The fear was still there...but at least I knew where I was coming from, where I was going, and what I was supposed to do with myself."

He made it. It was finished. He had attained the object of his obsession. Just a routine rappel down the wall, and he was free to move on to other things, pursuits considered more important and certainly safer by his family and friends. And then he heard footsteps.

Three men appeared, three fellow climbers at the top of El Cap who asked if they could rappel down first. They had been climbing for a long time and were eager to get down. Stopping meant falling asleep, so they needed to keep moving, if that was okay. "Who are these guys?" wondered Duane and his friends. As the first climber began his descent, Duane began a conversation with one of the others.

There was something about the man—a strength, an engaging quality, a confidence so strong it naturally pulled people in rather than drove them away. This was a man who had an intimate understanding of challenge and accomplishment.

"He was one of those rare men whose alpha status seems to emanate from their pores, their rank in any group somehow implicit, beyond question," is how Duane recalled him. Based on their obvious shared passion, the man took a genuine interest in Duane and his companions.

"What you boys been on?" he asked.

"Salathé," was Duane's response, proud in a modest sort of way.

"Oh, that's awesome. I've always wanted to do that route. Your first El Cap route?"

"Yeah."

"Right on. You guys must be feeling great. How long were you up there?"

"Five days."

"Right on. Congratulations. I've got to do the Salathé someday. Is it just great?"

"It's amazing. It was my fourth try though," said Duane as he began to suspect that his new friend was more than a little familiar with the many routes up El Cap and was no stranger to the top.

"Doesn't even matter. Everybody bails a few times. What matters is you made it. You ticked it."

"I guess so. What'd you guys just do?" Duane asked.

"Mescalito." Mescalito? No hint of boastfulness. No sign of one-upmanship. No rambling on about his climb and how good he felt. No pauses while he waited for the expressions of respect and awe to which he was entitled. Mescalito. And then Duane found out they had climbed right through the night, on the wall for twenty-eight straight hours.

Mescalito. It was one of those words that tells an informed person all he needs to know. Duane's suspicions were confirmed. It was climbing at a different level altogether. Duane had just summited El Capitan via the Salathé Wall, the climb of a lifetime, and he was reveling in that kind of exhausted satisfaction that saturates your entire soul. It's a feeling that many never experience in life. His previous failures made his success that much more rewarding. He had conquered his fears and accomplished what few people even try.

But Mescalito? Much harder and steeper than the Salathé. The man and his companions had accomplished something immeasurably more difficult in one-fifth the time. When Duane later discovered it was the man's fifty-second El Cap climb, he knew he had encountered the real deal. Mescalito. In twenty-eight hours. Fifty-second time on the summit. Duane was both reduced to insignificance and inspired to embrace even greater challenges.

"I had finally done the thing that was supposed to be the obstacle between me and the rest of my life, and now it appeared that the rest of a life could be devoted to the obstacle itself," said Daniel Duane.

It takes a climber years, not twenty-eight hours, to get to the top of El Cap, and there are no shortcuts. A person progresses from learning about the sport in a general way—the terms, equipment, and techniques—to specific instruction from a competent instructor, to top-roping. Top-roping, so named because the rope and anchor are always above the climber, is the entry point to actual climbing. It provides the security necessary to transfer the techniques a climber has learned mentally or in a gym to his physical performance outside. Top-roping allows a climber to focus on his climbing technique and the enjoyment of physical accomplishment.

As a climber learns and develops his skills, he begins to gain experience, both from climbing and from watching others climb. And as he gains experience, he hones his judgment and wisdom. When he can read a climb and has a solid skill set, he can put together efficient movement sequences so that his climb is not a series of fits and starts, but a smooth, confident, rhythmic progression.

Climbing is about movement, smooth and efficient actions that enable a climber to get from where he is to where he wants to go with the least amount of wear and tear. It's about attempting demanding climbs and having your imagination inspired. It's about moving from challenging, single-pitch climbs to multipitch routes and having your character developed along the way.

If a climber becomes comfortable with the gear, is competent in the fundamentals, and shows an interest in further development, he can partner with an experienced leader on a free climb. On a free climb, the lead climber is setting protection (the various pieces of equipment—carabiners, nuts, and spring-loaded camming devices —secured into the wall, through which the climbing rope is threaded) as he goes. Pitons, steel wedges or blades that are hammered into the rock, are rarely used today. Today's "pro" is much easier to place and, just as important, easier to remove. It violated the whole "leave no trace" ethos to pound spikes into a wall, especially if they were left behind. If the apprentice wants to continue his development even further, taking the role of leading a climb on an established route is the next step.

Ah, leading, being above your protection, taking the "sharp end of the rope," as they say. Rock climbing can be an unnerving sport. Leading a climb can be unnerving in a whole new way. As you climb, you glance up and all you see is rockface. You glance down, between your legs to the ground below, maybe far below, and all you see are the tops of trees, your belayer, and the protection you set along the way. Gone is the reassurance of the top rope. Gone is the simplicity of route choice. Gone is the freedom of climbing just for yourself.

Leading a first ascent is literally the pinnacle of climbing, the final frontier. You are leading the way to where no one has gone before. There are no guidebooks. You're making this up as you go, so you'd better know what you're doing. Climbing skill, route selection, judgment for the leader and his partner, wisdom and skill in placing protection, courage, resourcefulness, confidence, perseverance, and more come into play as never before.

"Leading is a thinking person's game: Where does this route go? What's my next protection going to be? Is my rope running straight and free of sharp edges and loose rock? Where's the next belay? Am I considering my second as I set up my protection on traverses? In other words, the leading game is multifaceted and all-absorbing, and you'll have to stay especially alert." Of course leading isn't just about controlling the variables, though you certainly need to plan for them. Leading is also about responding to the unexpected.

"I've had hornets up my shorts, been startled by a pigeon that brushed my face as it flew from its nest, stuck my fingers into the belly of a bat in a thin crack, surprised a snarling raccoon behind a flake on a high ledge and had my fixed rope chewed through by rats 2,500 feet up El Capitan," says climbing veteran Don Mellor. "Welcome to nature." There is no script.

Climbing in the United States took a big jump in the fifties and sixties. While most of the country was at home cozying up to the television, others went to Yosemite. And while some looked up at the granite faces and wondered if it could be done, men like Warren Harding, Royal Robbins, Chuck Pratt, Tom Frost, and Yvon Chouinard said, "I'll go first."

"Much of the difficulty in breaking through a barrier in any sport is largely psychological. The burden is always greater for the pioneer, who is in completely new territory and has no yardstick for comparison." Harding led the first ascent of El Capitan, taking forty-seven climbing days over a period of seventeen months. Someone's got to go first to show others that it can be done. The record today is less than four hours.

## LEADING THE MARRIAGE CLIMB

*Golgotha* is as meaningless as *Mescalito* to most people. But to those who knew what it took to get there, the one word says it all. Golgotha, the Place of the Skull, the place where Jesus was crucified. It is the place where history's most compelling teacher drove home His most emphatic point: If you want to be as I am, you must live as I live. If you want to live as I live, you must die as I died. And if you want to die as I died, you must also rise. It's living at a different level altogether.

Jesus was the breakthrough for us. He showed us life and relationships were possible in a whole new way—if we were willing to trust Him and do it His way. It wouldn't be easy. He came to serve, not to be served. Becoming more and more like Jesus is the goal of any Christian. It is the short-term goal, the midterm goal, and the long-term goal. It is the climb of our lives. Leadership means taking the initiative to lead that climb.

"Husbands, love your wives, just as Christ loved the church" (Ephesians 5:25) sets the bar pretty high. It's a challenge for men to assume leadership in the marriage. Not a rigid, "this is how it's going to be, this is where we're going" form of leadership, but a relentless, strong, dynamic, purposeful leadership toward attaining the character of Jesus.

Where Jesus started—absolute confidence in who He was, unwavering purposefulness, driven by a fiercely devoted, unconditional love—is where we want to end up. It is the wall we are climbing.

He was confident, not in ways that depend on accomplishment, acceptance, or approval. He simply knew who He was, and because of that, He did not regard equality with God as something to hold on to. He chose to take the first step and initiate the relationship with us. He lived a purposeful life of sacrificial love. He didn't worry about whether or not He would be treated "right" or if He got the credit He deserved.

And when people didn't respond as they should have or when Jesus didn't get the respect or credit to which He was entitled, He didn't pout. He didn't draw a line in the sand and say, "I will ___, if they will ___." He didn't withdraw from the relationship and say, "When they ___, then I can ___." He was laser locked on His purpose. He continued to initiate and develop relationships.

That is the model for the life Jesus calls us to. It is also our model for marriage. The first step is being confident enough in God, yourself, and the purpose to which He has called you that you can let go of entitlement. The second step is being so consumed by the purpose that you make an initial choice to obey and continue to choose obedience in the face of each day's challenges. It's the big picture being lived out frame by frame. And the third step is resurrection. When things don't go as you think they should, when you are hurt, when you don't get what you think you deserve, you rise from the disappointment and continue to pursue the purpose.

"Manhood means moving—not always success, not always victory, but moving, the kind of movement that only a passionate, consuming, Spirit-directed fascination with Christ can produce," says Larry Crabb in *God Calls Men to Move Beyond the Silence of Adam.*

## THE CHARACTER OF CHRIST

*Passionate, consuming, fascination*—strong words. If that doesn't describe our interest in Christ, maybe it's because we're afraid to look beyond the superficial images of Jesus as vaguely kind or sternly legalistic. Maybe we're more comfortable with easy images than the challenging reality. Read the Gospels, but forget that the story is about Jesus Christ—all caps, italicized, bold, underscored, the One who separated time into BC and AD. What characteristics do you see in Jesus the man? Who is this guy?

Put yourself in Jesus's shoes. Would you, as the son of a common laborer, be confident enough to get up in front of hundreds of people to go toe-to-toe with groups of religious professionals? And if you had the confidence, could you deliver? Would you be courageous enough to teach, knowing that the brightest, most powerful people in your society were using those opportunities to build a case for your execution?

If someone cast aside by society because of ethnicity, physical challenges, or moral shortcomings approached you with a genuine need that you could meet, would you hide behind excuses like busyness or your reputation as a community leader, or would you stop and meet the person's need? How poised would you be if confronted by two mentally ill men who were so violent that no one went near where they lived? Would you be so committed to your purpose you could not be deterred by the praise of crowds, threats of the government, or desertion by your closest friends? If you believed that the next step in pursuing your consuming life purpose meant you had to die, would you take the step?

As Christians, that's the way we are supposed to live. It's how we're supposed to approach work, relationships with friends and family, and recreational pursuits. But most especially, it's the way we are supposed to approach our married life. Unless you're consumed by a passion to get to the top, stay on the ground.

If you studied Tari and me, you would quickly conclude that she is a naturally gifted leader, much more so than I. She is confident, energetic, charismatic, and so genuinely interested in life and people that they are drawn to her. And regardless of what's going on in our lives at any particular time, "Okay, where do we go from here?" is never very far from the top of her mind.

Yet I'm convinced that I'm accountable for leading the way toward Christlikeness. That involves continuing to learn about His character and applying those lessons to my daily life. It also means establishing a relationship environment of acceptance, encouragement, serving one another in love, purposefulness, and more. We are each responsible for our own growth and how well we serve one another in love, but I feel I'm responsible for the tone of the relationship. Are we climbing toward serving one another in love and more purposeful lives, or are we slipping into patterns of self-serving behaviors?

I believe that discovering and living out who and what God made us to be is the best way to become more like Jesus. I lead by continuing to do that for myself and by encouraging and assisting Tari in her search. Whatever God has called and gifted a husband and wife to do with their lives—parenting, marketplace endeavors, ministry involvements—will be a huge part of their growth as individuals and as a couple.

## THE DEATH OF ENTITLEMENT

The fact that we are even aware of Jesus can be attributed to the fact that He did not regard equality with God as something to hold on to (Philippians 2:6). From the moment He became man until His crucifixion, His whole life personified the phrase "dying to self." He didn't have to do what He did, and He certainly was entitled to better than what He got. Entitlement. That's where Jesus started. No, not insisting on what He was entitled to, but letting go of it. He recognized that at best it is distraction. More likely, focusing on what you're entitled to, whether it's good or bad, is an aggressive form of relational cancer.

A lot of men lead, but they lead toward self-orientation. When they come to a particularly difficult pitch on their climb toward Christlikeness, if they're climbing at all, they make excuses and yield to some sort of entitlement. They withhold parts of themselves, giving of themselves only what they are most comfortable giving. Self-serving acts can be camouflaged as selfless acts of service. A tendency to manipulate and control can be disguised as strong leadership. A desire to gain approval can be made to look like servanthood.

"I deserve better than this" is one type of entitlement. We feel that we are entitled to better treatment than we are experiencing. We look at what good husbands we think we are, what good income earners we think we are, what good fathers we think we are, how well we compare to other husbands with conveniently obvious shortcomings, and we feel that our efforts justify more than we're getting. And maybe your efforts do merit more than you're getting—a more exciting life, a cleaner home, more frequent lovemaking, more time for yourself, more time for golf—whatever is important to you. You might be right. You may have a legitimate grievance.

The second type of entitlement that we feel is more personally judgmental. Things are not going as we hoped they would, and we blame ourselves or willingly accept the blame of our spouse: "This is exactly what I deserve. I should never expect better. This is my fault." We feel we are entitled to heap judgment on ourselves. It may look like accountability or humility, but it's really self-abuse. And it's where many people feel most comfortable.

But if Jesus is your model, you can forget about any sense of entitlement. He did. We simply can't imagine how great the discrepancy was between what He deserved and what He got.

Both forms of entitlement, being entitled to better treatment or deserving worse, keep us focused on ourselves and not on the best interests of our spouse or our marriage. It's the self-orientation we talked about earlier. You have no idea how often a sense of entitlement can come up until you are faced with a daily, intimate relationship like marriage. When we should be rising to the challenge of leading the climb toward becoming more like Jesus, we stand around dwelling on what we feel we deserve.

Jesus said that we demonstrate our love for Him not in some vague, conceptual way but in the day-to-day give-and-take of relationships. If we really love Him, then we actively care for others (John 21:15–17). Not some abstract other, but the real flesh-and-blood people in our lives. But He also warned that our love for Him needed to far exceed our love for anybody else, including our spouses or children.

If we choose to love Christ more than our spouses, we are freed from the desire to control or the need to earn their approval. We are freed from the fears of rejection or inadequacy. We are free to love our mates as Jesus would. We can ask, "What does this person need to move ahead in his or her journey toward Christlikeness?" It's a question of servanthood. We live as though the well-being of our spouses is the most important thing. Not their happiness. Not their approval. Not even our happiness. But their well-being.

## Who Goes First?

"Marriage cannot be successfully navigated without our giving more of ourselves than we are comfortable giving," say Henry Cloud and John Townsend. But many of us are afraid of the challenge, afraid of being exposed as inadequate. We're afraid that if we really invest ourselves in serving our spouses in love, we will see what a challenge it really is. We're also afraid of finding out that we're climbing alone, that maybe our mates aren't as committed to our needs as we'd hoped. And maybe they're not. They are afraid too. Afraid of being inadequate. Afraid of what happens if they get halfway up the rock's face and their partner quits, leaving them on the wall alone. Afraid that the person who has pursued them will find new and more interesting pursuits.

Many people are more willing to risk the relationship than themselves in the relationship.

Someone's got to go first. Someone's got to be willing to say, "I don't care who is entitled to what or who gets the credit. Christ was about serving, not being served. That's where I'm going. I may not know exactly how I'll get there, and I'm certain I'll fall and get discouraged, but I'm climbing." A husband has to be willing to take risks if he's going to move his marriage ahead. He has to take the sharp end of the rope. When it comes to serving one another in love, a husband can't afford to stand around at the base of the rock, pawing at the dirt with his shoe, and say to his wife, "Okay, you first." He has to take the lead.

Why the husband? That's what Jesus did.

In his book *Wild at Heart,* John Eldredge claims that a man is made to fight. He is not engaged until he is in a battle. And he is not fully engaged unless he is in a battle he isn't sure of winning. Though there are many worthy battles to fight, unless a man has first conquered his self-orientation, he is running from the real battle. And unless a husband has conquered self-orientation in his marriage, he hasn't really conquered it.

Jesus: confident and purposeful. Let go of any sense of entitlement. Initiated relationships and loved sacrificially. Not distracted by complacency, worried about inadequacy, or intimidated by threats. And when He didn't get the desired result or wasn't treated the way He was entitled to be treated, He didn't pout, judge, indulge self-pity, or put "if...then" conditions on His love. Though certainly hurt and disappointed, He simply rose and continued to do what He came to do. Over and over again, you see this pattern is Jesus's life. It is the route He chose and the route He calls us to, in life and in marriage.

All this love and sacrifice, what's it going to get you? A sense of entitlement to what you've earned or a spirit of resentment for what you've given up, unless...unless you're willing to focus on what you're becoming, not what you're getting.

The character of Christ is what we should be getting. It is the goal toward which we are climbing. It is who you are becoming in the marriage process, and it is a big unknown. Marriage is the big wall you've chosen to climb in order to get to the top. It is your first ascent. Each day is new. Each day you climb. Each day you lead. Which direction you lead is up to you.

## SUMMARY

The concept of leadership in a marriage is an area of great debate in the church. And the idea of the man taking the lead in establishing a relationship environment runs against our normal cultural training.

Perhaps because of those reasons, it is important that as a couple you decide what you believe about leadership in your relationship. I believe that the man is most responsible for leading the climb toward Jesus's character, especially in serving one another in love.

## For Reflection

1. Do you agree that the man is primarily responsible for setting the tone of the relationship?
2. On a day-to-day basis in your life and your marriage, what does leading the climb toward Christlikeness look like for you?

# There's a Reason They Call It Terminal Velocity

## committing to marriage is like skydiving

> *Whatever you do, don't try to hold on to the door*
> *if you change your mind, because I'll break your arms.*
> *"No, no, no" sounds a lot like "Go, go, go."*
>
> BEN CROWELL, tandem skydiving leader

fter exiting the aircraft…"

If you've ever taken a commercial flight, you know you're about to be told where to get your bags. And after waiting for what seems like forever for everyone in the rows ahead of you to get items "that may have shifted during the flight" from the overhead compartments, you trudge up the aisle, step out of the plane, and walk down the Jetway. It's the most common way of exiting a plane. Not much fun and little is required in the way of commitment, but it's nice to be back on the ground.

There is a faster way out of a plane, but it does require a little more preparation and a lot more commitment. You can jump. Not from a commercial plane of course, but from a small private plane specially adapted for skydiving. Skydiving is an all-or-nothing deal. A person who does exit an aircraft in this manner will find it much more helpful to concentrate on doing the necessary things to land safely than to entertain doubts about the wisdom of the endeavor. A few thousand feet above some farmer's field is not the place to wonder about the jumpmaster's qualifications, the thoroughness of the rigger who packed your chute, or whether or not you should go through with this. The commitment has been made.

Unlike the passenger who strolls down the Jetway, a person who jumps will accelerate for nine to twelve seconds. At that point, the air resistance catches up to the pull of gravity. Terminal (final, not fatal) velocity they call it. About 120 miles per hour. If the skydiver wants to, he can tuck his arms to his side, tip forward, and *really* fly. A more streamlined shape means less resistance, and less resistance means more speed. Maybe 200 miles per hour. And he will remain pretty much at that speed until something changes, like his position, the deployment of a parachute, or a sudden encounter with the ground. Terminal velocity can also be fatal.

Every year thousands of people jump for the first time. Most are tandem jumpers. In a tandem jump, the first-timer is attached to an experienced jumper who is certified, not only to step out of a plane and into the sky himself, but also to step out while attached to someone else. Another one of those two-have-become-one deals. To be certified as a tandem instructor, a jumper must have logged five hundred jumps, been in the sport for at least two years, and have completed a tandem instruction class. Clearly, this is a person who knows what he's doing. At least they have until now. No reason to believe that will change, right?

"In a tandem jump, the student can just relax and enjoy the ride down," is what they tell you at the skydiving center. Sure, relax. Nothing to this falling from nearly three miles up in the sky.

Step out of the plane and into the sky. Nothing to it. Few actions in our daily lives are more common than taking a step, but no step is as committed as the one taken by a tandem instructor with a first-time skydiver attached. It's a step and a process unlike any other.

Everyone's different. But as diverse as first-time skydivers are, they all have one thing in common—nervousness. It may run from mild anxiousness to full-blown what-have-I-gotten-myself-into panic. But you will feel squeamish at some point.

The nervousness may start the week before your jump. You're going about your normal activities and then remember that this weekend, or whenever you've scheduled your jump, will be anything but normal. In a few days you'll be paying someone to push you out of a plane. Nothing normal about that. Your nervousness may ebb and flow, creeping up into acute awareness and then falling away as the demands of each day regain your attention. Maybe you'll reassure yourself with Jesus's teaching that each day has enough worry of its own.

Or maybe the short prejump class will suddenly make the risk real. Oh sure, they show you the video of people excitedly spilling out of a plane and into the sky, having such an obvious blast that you wonder why skydiving isn't part of every high school gym class. And the instructor will reassure you that the person you are jumping with is at least as interested as you in pulling this thing off. He'll tell you that if you get swept up in the excitement of the jump and forget to pull the rip cord (very likely), your tandem instructor will do it. He'll tell you that even if your instructor passes out or goes into a brain freeze so inexplicably complete that he doesn't pull the rip cord, the automatic deployment device (if the jump center has them) will deploy the chute. So intellectually you know this is safe, but still…

So maybe the week before your jump passes in a busy blur. Perhaps you go through class and gear up with the eagerness of a child winding through a line at an amusement park ride, drawing ever-closer to the ride itself. Maybe your nervousness will hit you as you're walking out to the plane. There's something very reassuring about feeling the ground under your feet and knowing that the movements you are making are an act of your own will. But you know that with each step, you're that much closer to the plane. And the only reason you're even walking to the plane is so you can jump out of it.

Perhaps the nervousness will kick in once you're belted into your seat and the pilot starts the engines. He'll glance over the instruments, make sure everyone's settled in back, check the ground around the plane and the skies overhead, then taxi to the end of the runway. It starts to dawn on you that you have set in motion a sequence of events that are beyond your control.

Now you're moving without moving. You experience the same

thing every time you're in a car, but you're familiar with cars. You can always stop a car. And you've probably never jumped out of one, not while it was moving at a hundred miles per hour. It's amazing how acutely aware you become of what's going on around you when you know that every change and every little action mean one thing—you're that much closer to the single step that is the biggest leap of faith you will ever take.

The pilot revs the engine, checking it and the propellers. Kind of odd when you think about it, but he's making sure that the plane you will soon be abandoning is safe. He scans the sky for other aircraft, then turns onto the active runway. He pushes the throttle forward, and the plane accelerates, as does your imagination. A few seconds later you feel the nose go up, and the wheels leave the runway. Your familiar horizontal world is suddenly vertical.

Unless you're preternaturally calm or have the presence of mind to focus on the task, some pretty strange what-ifs can pop up. Your instructor will chat you up, trying to relax a mind that may be clamped shut in fear. He'll remind you to squat in the doorway of the plane, like a catcher in baseball. He'll remind you to arch back into him in a complete legs-spread, arms-extended spread eagle once you've jumped. He'll remind you of the midair adjustments he'll make that will loosen the connections just a little. He'll tell you to keep your eyes open because it's really cool to watch the plane as you jump from it. He'll also tell you to breathe and have fun. And he will do all this over the steady drone of the engine.

For the next few minutes, you'll be doing whatever it is you do when you're involved in a bold, new adventure. (Let's not call it feeling scared.) Maybe you'll chatter away or laugh nervously. Perhaps you'll silently stare out the window at good old mother earth, speaking only when spoken to and then in single syllables. Yes, good old, steadily-dropping-farther-away mother earth. But hey, one way or another, you'll be back on the ground in no time.

You may think about all your "whuffo" friends back on the ground, the ones who wanted to know, "Whuffo they jump out of airplanes?" You may wonder yourself about the wisdom of your decision and how stupid you'd feel if you tapped the instructor on the shoulder and shouted, "Sorry, changed my mind." If it could be done discreetly, perhaps you'd do it. But you would have to shout over all the noise, and somehow your fears are not something you want to shout about. Besides, that's what the first few seconds of the jump are for. By the way, did you use the bathroom before you went up?

To the pilot and the instructor, who have done this many times before, it's just another first jump. But this is unlike any other first jump, because it is *your* first jump. And it is the only first jump you will ever have. You'd like to get it right. Getting it wrong means… well, you'd really like to get it right.

After about ten or twelve minutes of inactivity when you've tried not to think about the staggering significance of what you're about to do, your instructor begins final preparations. He'll remind you to wear your goggles (like your eyes are going to be open, right?). He will clip his harness, the one with the parachute, to yours, the one without. Two will become one. For better or worse. In sickness or in health. For the next few minutes, your lives are inextricably inter-twined. It may occur to you that you know virtually nothing about this person who is about to push you out of a plane.

After about fifteen minutes of climbing, the pilot will turn the plane into the wind once again, and a green light will come on. Time to go. Someone will slide the door open. Expect a sensory burst as the cool wind and the smell of the engine suddenly rushes in. Expect that it will be hard to hear—between the sounds of the wind, the engine, and the kettle-drum pounding of your heart. It may be hard to think, too, because you realize that the door is open for one reason: this little plane you are now in is soon to become the little plane you used to be in.

You are about to take the single most significant step you have ever taken. You know that statistically it's not risky. Of all the thou-sands of jumps each year, on average only thirty-three people die. Your confidence should be buoyed by the knowledge that, on aver-age, a parachutist will go 333 jumps between main-chute malfunc-tions. Since this is your first, you're a lock. The odds are in your favor. What could go wrong, right?

The instructor will probably give you a little pep talk and review the essentials. He may conclude with something like, "I've got you. You'll do great. Now, you ready?" You may wonder if you would be construed as fearful if you suddenly dropped to the floor of the plane, wrapped yourself around the instructor's leg, and pleaded, "No. No, I'm not ready. Don't make me go through with this. I'm definitely *not* ready."

Any experienced jumpers on the flight will precede you out of the plane. Up from their seats and out of the plane. See, it's okay. See how much fun all the others are having? But then your turn rolls around. Clipped to your instructor, you scoot, hop, slide toward that open door. Wow, what a great view! Intersecting country roads. Flat fields. Maybe the tops of some cottony clouds. Small towns. Maybe off in the distance a major metropolitan area.

If you've made it through the week and all the prejump preparation without much nervousness, this is when you can expect a full-blown "What was I thinking?" deluge of anxiousness. You try to calm yourself (*He knows what he's doing…I'm pretty sure. The system is safe…at least it has been until now.*) because you might need to be clearheaded, and you want to enjoy the day. Faith and fear in a cage match.

You're clinging to this last bit of what feels like security. You're in your catcher's squat at the open door of a plane, prop blast racing past, traveling at a hundred miles an hour, nearly three miles above the ground, with about 270 pounds of instructor and equipment clipped to your back, but you feel secure. Sort of. At least physically. Relative to how you're going to feel in a few seconds, anyway.

This is the moment you've waited for or maybe hoped would never arrive. You know your life will never be the same, assuming of course that all goes well and you still have a life. All that separates you from the thrill of your first jump or the blind terror of falling through the sky is a single step.

"Lean forward, and don't forget your arch," your instructor tells you as he begins a gentle rock toward the door. "Ready. Set. Go." Suddenly you're tumbling out of the plane and into the sky. You arch your back, raise your head, and spread your arms and legs, just as they told you in class.

*Yeeeeeeehaaaaaaah!* You are free-falling. You did it! You'll have about sixty seconds to enjoy the euphoric combination of adrenaline and airspeed. Then you, if you remember, or your instructor will pull the handle. You will feel a tug at your shoulders as you are pulled upright and a jolt of excitement as you quickly slow down from about 120 miles per hour to about 20. You look up at the canopy spread above you and down at the ground below. It worked! There's still a long way to go, but for a moment, this quiet, pristine moment, you have done what few people are willing to do, and the sky is yours to enjoy.

## The Marital Leap of Faith

There is only one way to know the thrill of a first jump—commit. Jump! And there is only one way to know the thrill of a successful marriage. Commit! Commit to the action, not just to the idea. Jump! It's not as easy as it sounds. It is simple, but not easy.

A successful marriage is like going through three doors of commitment. You cannot have a successful extreme marriage without going through all three, shutting them behind you, and locking them. The first commitment is that divorce is not an option. You are committed to staying married. If you don't make this commitment, you will spend a lot of time and emotional energy entertaining thoughts and considering alternatives that are counterproductive to what you say you want. It's a huge step, an important step, but it is only the first door. Some people make this commitment, then refuse to rise further to the challenge of a growing marriage. For them, staying together is the marriage commitment.

Many people will stay together for financial reasons, for social or family reasons, for professional reasons, or for the benefit of the children. Regardless of the quality of their married life or their motivations, they feel they have met their obligation by staying together. They stay together, but you wonder, what's the point? They go through the motions of marriage, settling for meeting the obligation instead of pursuing genuine connection.

But you know a lot of couples who have divorced, probably even appear to be better off divorced. Many people come from a home environment in which divorce was a relief from the constant fighting, tension, or just indifference. Divorce was an option, one that everyone involved seemed to benefit from.

That's because many people haven't made the second commitment. A lousy or even mediocre marriage is not an option either. Most of us want a great marriage. Maybe we're even committed to an excellent relationship. We're simply not going to settle for anything less. Why get married if you don't want one? It's another good, necessary step. But again, it is only one door.

What happens if you start to feel you don't have a great marriage? If you haven't made the first commitment, this second one could present a challenge. You want to have a great marriage but may realize you don't want one with the person you are married to. Maybe you think you'll never be able to have a great marriage with this person—not a bad person, just a bad choice for you. You may start to think about moving on. Give each of you a chance to start over, to make a better choice next time. If your commitment to the ideal of a happy marriage is stronger than your commitment to the reality of your marriage, you may bail.

The third commitment is to do the work of an excellent marriage. Now you're talking. You've made the commitment to stay. You're not going anywhere. And you've made the commitment that a lousy or even a mediocre marriage is unacceptable. You've seen those and it scares you. You're afraid it could be you—bored, frustrated, just going through the motions. That's not for you either. So you slam those first two doors behind you and lock them. If you've committed to what's not going to happen, you have no choice but to commit to do the work of an extreme marriage. You are going to pay whatever price is necessary to make yours a success.

## YOUR IMPERFECT DECISION

Commitment is so important because regardless of how thorough and well-informed your decisions were, many things won't be revealed until you are in the crucible of marriage. When you marry, you are making a decision to accept that person as he or she is right now. That person is a package of good and bad. Most of it you know about, at least you hope you do. But some you don't. You've both kept things hidden. Some things you intentionally hid. You don't want them known now or ever. Some things you just didn't know.

You cannot know everything you need to know to make a perfect decision. As a matter of fact, there is no such thing as a perfect decision. You, as an imperfect person, made an imperfect decision to marry an imperfect person. As you go through life together, your imperfections are likely to become more apparent to each other, not less. You will learn new things about yourself and your spouse in marriage. Some of them you'll refuse to acknowledge. Some of them you'd rather not know. Some of them will make your life more difficult than you think it should be. Some of them you won't understand. It may be the first year, the fifth year, or the twentieth year. Changes need to be made. Growth needs to happen. In you and your spouse.

"Commitment provides the time, structure and security needed for change to take place," say Henry Cloud and John Townsend.

Down the road you may think, *Well, if I had known about (fill in the blank), I never would have married this person,* or, *I knew about this. We should have worked this out before the wedding.* "I woulda/shoulda/coulda…" and "If only I had known…" are potentially fatal distractions in marriage. First of all, you might not have married your spouse, but you would have made a similarly imperfect decision with a different imperfect person and be thinking the same thoughts. Second, your partner may be coming to some "If only I had known…" conclusions too.

Either way, it doesn't make any difference because new information should challenge your resourcefulness, not your commitment. Have you been thorough and purposeful enough in your dating over a long enough period of time to make that kind of commitment?

## WHATEVER HAPPENED TO COMMITMENT?

Somewhere along the line, society's definition of commitment shifted. Much like the word *love,* its meaning has been watered down. To some people a commitment means to try really, really hard. A commitment to try is an escape clause. And if there is an escape clause, many people will take it when the going gets tough, which it always does, even if only for a season of life. If you try hard and get a disappointing result, well at least you tried hard. To others, commitment means something you can't get out of. It's like gum on your shoe, an annoyance that is easier to put up with than to do something about. That won't cut it in extreme marriage.

A decision is not necessarily a commitment. There will be times when you question your decision. There will be times when you think the work is too hard, your differences too great, your individual issues too strong, the rut you're stuck in too deep and getting deeper by the day. You want to quit. Maybe your spouse wants to quit. Many people would understand if you said to them that you were quitting. But you made a commitment; at least you think you did. You know you made a decision.

You don't really know whether the decision you made is also a commitment until you want to quit. Your responses to the challenges of life and your marriage will reveal whether you made a commitment or a decision.

I know firsthand how critical commitment is to the success of a marriage. I was married before. I didn't have the skills I needed (the skills discussed in this book) to make my marriage a success. *Nobody* has all the necessary skills. There are just too many variables over too much time.

But more crucial than the skills I didn't have was the attitude I lacked. If I'd had the right attitude, I could have developed the necessary skills. I went into marriage thinking that divorce was not an option for me. I made a marriage decision. In retrospect, I can see I didn't make a marriage commitment.

When my marriage bogged down due to a lack of vision, ignorance of how I needed to grow, and a poor relationship work ethic, I quit. That's embarrassing to admit. But the disillusionment and pain I experienced as a result of that failure has led me to an entirely different level of commitment. And that commitment has enabled me to learn the skills, confront my own challenges, and address the issues that Tari and I encounter even today after eleven years of marriage.

It's a comedic cliché, but many of us are afraid of the commitment of marriage. Maybe we understand at our core that a successful marriage isn't about business as usual. Maybe we have a sense that more will be required of us than we are accustomed to giving.

Probably much more. And we don't know if we can do it. We don't know if anyone can do it. It's very possible we've never seen a marriage we want to emulate.

Most of us don't know what we're really capable of until it is asked of us. Or more likely, demanded of us. If we are committed to the effort but not the result, we are more likely to give what we want to give or think we can give, not what is required to accomplish the goal.

Success in marriage requires the same commitment as success in extreme sports. You have to push yourself. To get better you have to give more of yourself than you did before. And who doesn't want to get better? Jumping out of an airplane for the first time is a huge rush, even if your tandem instructor, not you, pulls the rip cord. But tandem jumping quickly becomes dull. You want to jump for yourself. You want to free-fall farther. You want to develop.

Do you have all the skills necessary to have a successful extreme marriage?

Definitely not. Can you develop them? Yes, you can. With Christ's help you can, but probably won't. Until you make the commitments that you're going to stay and that a mediocre marriage is not an option. Everyone wants an excellent marriage, but most people aren't aware of the growth price they will have to pay. Or maybe they are aware but choose to not pay it. They don't believe the payoff is worth the investment. This kind of commitment is a huge price. It is also a necessary price for a successful marriage.

That's when I began to develop as a spouse. But even after I'd made those commitments, I couldn't have done it without the life-changing power of a relationship with Christ. Without that relationship I wouldn't have had the honesty to admit my short-comings, the humility to seek out new ideas, the wisdom to know how to apply them to myself and my marriage, the strength to per-severe in the growth process, and the grace and love to extend to Tari.

And that's when my skills began to catch up to the challenges. That's when the adventure really began.

We'd all feel differently about our dating process and marriage ceremony if the processional at the beginning of the service was not a slow, graceful entrance by a beautiful bride but a tandem jump with a parachute packed by our spouse. You're sure he or she knows how to do this, right? If not, that's going to be a pretty quick four-teen thousand feet. Of course you know what you're doing, right? I mean, no questions there. Thumbs up. Green light. It's a go, right?

There are two approaches to skydiving. One is to stay safely on the ground. Many people can't understand why anyone would ever jump out of a perfectly good aircraft. Or they understand, and it sure looks like fun but definitely for someone else. That's not neces-sarily bad. It is wise when people know their tolerance for adventure and stick to it.

The other approach is to get in the plane, go up in the sky, and jump. What a blast! Generally, people in the first group are not up in the plane.

Unfortunately, the same is not true in marriage. Many of the people in the first group are up in the plane. They're married, but they haven't committed. They may be in the plane, kneeling at the open door, ready to go. It's noisy. They are getting beaten by the propeller wash. They want to jump. The concept sure made sense. It looked like great fun when they were on the ground. But when they are the ones poised to jump, they are scared to death to take the step.

You will face the same two choices in marriage. You can choose what seems like safety and either stay on the ground or freeze when it's your turn to go. But there's a huge cost in choosing safety. You'll never know what's possible unless you commit to the risk and embrace the adventure. Safety or adventure—you will choose one or the other.

## Summary

Commitment is the attitude that undergirds your entire relationship. A commitment to Christ. A commitment to stay in the marriage. A commitment that mediocrity is not an option. And finally, a commitment to pay whatever growth price is necessary to move the relationship ahead.

## For Reflection

1.  What endeavor or relationship is the best example of commitment in your life?

2.  What specific actions demonstrate your commitment to that endeavor or relationship?

3.  What lessons from skydiving can you apply to your marriage?

# It's not about the Bike, really

## Growing through ineffective Relationship Patterns is like Preparing for a stage Race in cycling

*Mountain days it [the handlebar computer] comes off,*
*since everything that weighs above five grams comes off.*

LANCE ARMSTRONG, six-time winner of the Tour de France

Today his chest is as featureless and uninspiring as the plains of his native Texas. His pipestem arms hang from bony shoulders. His stomach is flat, not rippled with muscles. In a world in which even marginal athletes are increasingly chiseled, there is nothing about his upper body that suggests he is in an elite category. At five feet eleven and 165 pounds with 4 percent body fat, you'd think of him as skinny if you passed him on the street. But it wasn't always that way.

"I was built like a linebacker," he recalls, "with a thick neck and slabs of muscle in my chest, remnants of my career as a swimmer and triathlete." Okay, he also admits to some "puppy fat" and maybe an extra pound or two from indulging a fondness for margaritas and tortilla chips. But he was fit and strong, and his strength served him well. He was beginning to have some successes but was inconsistent. A friend told him he needed to lose weight if he ever wanted to win his sport's most prestigious event. In a sport as specialized as his, the extra mass was a liability, not an asset. The challenge was to lose weight but maintain the strength he would need to win that event, a three-week, two-thousand-plus-mile race.

In a multiday bicycle stage race that includes ascents in the mountains, an obvious downside of weight is the energy required to haul it around or, more accurately, haul it up. He had a simple success formula: "Measure the weight of the body, the weight of the bike, and the power of the legs. Make the weight go down and the power go up." Losing weight is the easy part. The idea is to lose excess weight but maintain strength and stamina. "If you weighed too little, you wouldn't have the physical resources to generate enough speed," he cautioned. On the other hand, "If you weighed too much, your body was a burden. It was a matter of power to weight."

He not only lost the weight, about twenty pounds, but he kept it off. I suppose when a guy nicknamed "the Cannibal" tells you to trim down, you listen. And when the Cannibal is a five-time winner of that coveted race, an event you have never even finished, you listen closely. In the next race, things would be different, very different. He had no way of knowing how different.

He began the race by winning the brief but important prologue in record-breaking time. He added a stage victory a few days later in a time trial he won by fifty-eight seconds. After two weeks he was leading the race by two minutes and twenty seconds, but ahead lay the mountains with "peaks that made riders crack like walnuts." In the mountains the race would be won or lost; there those with a real shot at winning separated themselves from the merely good. Always has been and always will be. He had never been known as a climber, and most people expected him to be one of those who cracked.

The first mountain stage included three big peaks. He and his teammates rode well up the first peak. At the top of the second, the tallest at over eighty-six hundred feet, it was sleeting and raining. Less than ideal conditions, way less. But you pick the race, not the conditions under which the race is held. And remember, unknown challenges are part of the adventure. Then came the descent.

"You hunch over your handlebars and streak seventy miles an hour on two small tires a half-inch wide, shivering," is how he recalls the trip down the mountain. "Now throw in curves, switchbacks, hairpins, and fog. Water streamed down the mountainside under my wheels." It was treacherous. Behind him, the teammate who had led him up the mountain crashed.

On to the next peak, the third in six hours, and into more freezing rain and mist, alone this time, without a teammate to pace him or draft behind. At the summit, the rain froze to his jersey. It hailed on the way down. On to the final nineteen-mile climb to the stage's finish. With only five miles remaining, he was in a pack of four other riders, thirty-two seconds behind the two leaders. Time to see what he and everyone else had left, to see if his weight loss and hard work would pay off.

On a small curve, he cut to the inside, stood up, and accelerated. Nobody matched him. He quickly cleared the pack of elite climbers and made up twenty-one seconds on the two leaders. It felt strangely effortless. The weight loss and training were paying off. But he still had more than four miles to go and was still back by eleven seconds. Plenty of time to crack. Instead, he continued to close. He caught the leaders. Time to see what they had left.

"I surged again," he recalls, "driving the pace just a little higher. I was probing, seeking information on their fitness and states of mind, how they would respond." They didn't respond. They couldn't.

"Why don't you put a little more on," said his coach into the radio transmitter. He accelerated again and the gap widened. But now, his coach told him, one of the other riders was beginning a surge of his own. The chaser was about to become the chased.

"Look, I'm just going to go," he said to his coach. "I'm going to put this thing away." He did, accelerating again. He was never caught and won the stage, widening his overall lead to three minutes and three seconds. He widened his lead further the next day with another strong climb. He wasn't cracking. He wouldn't crack. He would go on to win the race. It was the first of six consecutive Tour de France victories for the leaner, lighter Lance Armstrong.

As his friend Eddy "the Cannibal" Merckx had recommended, Armstrong lost the weight. Of course, testicular cancer and the treatments associated with it weren't part of the weight-loss program Merckx had in mind.

Extra weight is a cyclist's enemy. It not only requires more energy to move, it also increases something called rolling resistance. Bicycles slow down because of friction, and rolling resistance is the second most significant source of friction. We don't usually think about it, but as a wheel rolls, it temporarily compresses against the surface it is on, slightly flattening out. When that happens, friction is created and energy is lost. The greater the weight of the rider and the cycle, the more vertical force pressing down on the tire as it contacts the surface, and the greater the rolling resistance. Anything that reduces the surface area contact between the tire and road will also reduce the amount of resistance and subsequently increase a cyclist's speed. Thin, properly inflated tires with smooth treads and strong sidewalls mean decreased surface contact and less energy wasted. Something else you don't think about is the energy you lose to the moving parts of the process. Friction among the bearings accounts for an estimated 1 percent loss, chain friction another 1.5–5 percent. And there is even a certain amount of power lost to friction in that most complex of machines, the human body. Joint friction takes another 2 percent of a cyclist's power output. Those may not seem like significant numbers, but in a three-week, two-thousand-mile race like the Tour, any inefficiency could be the one that costs a rider a victory. As Armstrong says and Greg LeMond knows, every second counts. LeMond, the only other American ever to win the Tour, finished second in 1985, a mere one minute and forty-two seconds behind the winner. Close, but not as close as his 1989 victory, which he won by a microscopic eight seconds. Every second does count, and so does every ounce.

But by far the biggest source of friction is the resistance of the air to the unified mass of the cyclist and his bike. This resistance is known as drag. The bike accounts for about 30 percent of the total drag. That's important in a sport where advantages are gained by the ounce and second, but it's not as important as the 70 percent drag contributed by the rider's body. Everyone agrees that Armstrong was right; it's not about the bike. So how does a rider reduce drag? "Using an aero bar with elbow rests (instead of a standard drop model) lowers drag more than any other modification," say the editors of *Bicycle Magazine.* Aero bars are basically an extra set of handlebars that extend forward from the stem. Compared to a rider using only the more traditional drop-down handlebars, a rider using an aero bar naturally assumes a lower, more streamlined riding posture as he leans forward and down, his forearms and hands extending away from his body and over the wheel. The idea is to present a narrow, compact, efficiently moving, relatively unified whole for the air to slip past with as little resistance as possible.

None of this feels natural. Your arms feel way too close together. Since you've intentionally narrowed yourself, you don't feel as balanced. And you'll have to fight the urge to keep popping your head up for a look around. It may take weeks or even months of gradual adjustments for a cyclist to feel comfortable with these changes.

When you were a kid with energy to burn and only riding over to your friend's house to play, you didn't care about rolling resistance, drag, or efficiency. Speed, yes. Efficiency, no. Lance Armstrong was probably no different. But in the world of stage cycling, factors like reducing drag, weight, and rolling resistance go a long way toward achieving success. And the same is true in marriage.

## A FEW EXTRA POUNDS IN YOUR RELATIONSHIP

We all come into marriage carrying a few extra pounds. This extra weight is the relationship patterns we have developed that are more about our self-orientation than serving one another in love. It's the ways we have learned to get by in relationships, to have relationships in ways that are easiest or most beneficial for us. It might be a little or it might be a lot, but all of us carry some excess weight. And unfortunately, our tendency is to pick up a little more.

Much of what we learned about ourselves, relationships in general, and marriage specifically was "taught" to us before we even realized we were learning, by people who didn't realize they were teaching and may not have been qualified to teach in the first place.

"Everyone who has ever lived has encountered a particular problem: being born a little person in a big person's world and being given the task of becoming a big person over time," says Dr. Henry Cloud. "We are all born children under adult authority, and over time we are to become authorities ourselves and be in charge of our lives." It's the process of bonding and separation, forming relationships and being part of a system, and at the same time being an autonomous individual apart from those connections. This is the normal expectation of normal children born into and nurtured by normal, loving families. Dr. David Stoop gets into the specifics of this normal process in his book *Forgiving Our Parents, Forgiving Ourselves.*

> Our first task in life—the first job we set out upon, even before we are old enough to consciously know what we are doing—is to form an attachment with a figure who will make the world a safe and reliable place for us. Ordinarily, of course, this is the mother, though the father also plays a crucial role.... Our second task in life is to define ourselves as separated, unique individuals within this context of love and trust. This is sometimes referred to as "individuation," the process of discovering what it is that "makes me, me." Our ability to accomplish this second task will be directly related to how much love and security we have experienced in the earlier process of bonding with our parents and our environment.
>
> Since unconditional love is the basis for all that occurs at later stages, we can round out our definition of the normal family by saying that it is a place where we can experience an unconditional love that gives us both the security and the freedom to successfully become autonomous individuals.

Of course, that may be so far from the experience of most of us that it sounds like it's from another planet altogether. Down here, things ain't so "normal." We are the imperfect offspring of the imperfect union of two imperfect people, all of which forms an imperfect immediate family, which is just a link in the chain of generations of imperfect families. And every variable in this equation of imperfection has been subject to the influence of an imperfect world. That's not a judgment. Imperfection doesn't mean that we, our parents, our families, or our world are necessarily bad.

Everyone's experience is different, but one thing is consistent: we never had a chance at the ideal that Stoop discusses. None of us. Our developmental process has fallen short of that ideal. It's the way things work in a fallen world. It is what it is. But once we recognize what it is and accept that, regardless of how fallen it is, we still have the responsibility and opportunity to grow and become better spouses. We can make the necessary adjustments.

Armstrong didn't win the Tour because he lost weight. He put himself in a much better position to win. But he still had to train. More important, he still had to go out and ride in the race. And not just ride, but ride better than all the other cyclists. He had to do the work of a champion if he was going to know the thrill of being a champion.

To help us recognize what we are up against, Cloud has identified common difficulties that have resulted from falling short of the ideal. These are areas of difficulty that all of us, to one degree or another, struggle with. And they can all be traced back to the failure of our families to meet that ideal. Even though we are free-to-choose adults now, these initial relationship difficulties continue to plague us until we take specific steps to address them and improve our own relationships.

## THE CHALLENGE OF BONDING WITH OTHERS

The first difficulty Cloud identifies is *bonding with others.* "Bonding is the ability to establish an emotional attachment with others." It's usually easy, though perhaps conflicted (from "I never knew I could love someone so much" to "Wow, is he ever going to stop crying?") for parents and a newborn. However, as the months and years pass and the relationship develops, the variables increase and the history grows. Healthy and lasting bonding is not easy. Much like marriage itself, the ease of the early relationship fades and is replaced by the need for relationship skills.

In our families, not only are we learning relationship skills, we are also learning values and attitudes. Attitudes that we have about ourselves and our parents increasingly come into play. And so do their attitudes about themselves and us. When the bonding is positive and healthy, we develop a trusting relationship of love with our parents that encourages a strong self and the beginnings of acquiring the skills necessary to become autonomous adults.

When the bonding is negative, neglected, or just incomplete, we can develop numerous symptoms like meaninglessness, emptiness, sadness, addictions, fantasies, and fears of intimacy, to name a few. You can see the results of ineffective bonding all around you, in your friends, your work associates, your brothers and sisters, probably your spouse, and maybe, if you look really closely, yourself.

## The Challenge of Separating from Others

The second difficulty Cloud identifies is *separating from others.* We spend much of our early lives unquestioningly belonging to our families, absorbing values and attitudes, learning the rules, if not the underlying principles. At some point we start to question and begin the process of becoming more of our own person. It may be a period of outright rebellion. It's certainly a time of transition as the parent-child relationship continues to evolve. We begin to understand that we have choices. We don't have to think, feel, or behave in ways that are acceptable to our parents. There may be consequences for not conforming to their expectations, but that is a choice we can and do make.

At the heart of separating are boundaries. "In the simplest sense, a boundary is a property line. It denotes the beginning and end of something," explain Cloud and Townsend. There are things inside the boundary that you can control and are responsible for, and things that are outside the boundary that you can't control and aren't responsible for. The most obvious and easiest-to-understand boundary is our body. Our skin wraps up our muscles, tissue, and organs into one package, a physical boundary. We learn how to control our body and discover that we are responsible for its actions. There are other, less obvious boundaries. Our attitudes, thoughts, desires, feelings, and abilities are examples of things inside our boundaries that we have control over and are responsible for. But of all the things within our boundaries, choices are the most significant.

"Choices are the foundation upon which boundaries are built," says Cloud. "But our choices are not true choices unless we are aware of all the aspects of our identity that go into them—our feelings, attitudes, behaviors, wants, and thoughts." The choices we make are a reflection of how effective our bonding has been, how well we've learned important relationship skills, and how strong our sense of self is.

Boundaries define the physical, psychological, and emotional people we are. At the heart of boundaries is ownership. We own what's ours to own. We take responsibility for our thoughts, attitudes, behaviors, and all the rest. And we also take responsibility for their consequences. And equally important, we don't own what's not ours to own. We're not responsible for the attitudes, feelings, and behaviors of others or their consequences. No relationship pattern is more destructive than to try to make choices for someone else or to try to let someone make choices for us. Ultimately we still make the choice, but we attempt to shift responsibility to another person, a person who is more powerful or whose willingness to determine our choices appears to make our lives easier. It is the old path of least resistance, the self-orientation thing. We want relationships (that's a God-given need), but we want them in ways that are easiest for us.

Accepting responsibility for the actions and attitudes of others, whether we reach for it ourselves or allow it to be thrown onto us, is as counterproductive for a husband or wife as being overweight is for a cyclist. We might be able to get away with it on the relatively easy, flat stages of early relationship, but on the climbs and descents of the tougher mountain stages, like parenting and long-term relationship, the extra weight will kill you.

Armstrong says that as a result of the lost weight, he is three minutes faster over a mountain pass, probably twelve minutes faster over a typical mountain stage. In case you're wondering, his margin of victory in his first Tour win was seven minutes and thirty-nine seconds. It was also his widest margin. His closest? Sixty-one seconds in 2003.

Generally, the healthier the bonding has been with both parents, the easier separation will be for everyone. But things can get fouled up when patterns are established in childhood that people continue to live out as adults. The lessons we internalized, the skills we developed, and our resulting way of approaching the world might have been mostly positive and productive—or negative and hurtful. One thing we know for sure, they weren't perfect and aren't complete. But you get to a point when you have to make decisions for yourself about whether or not those ways will be your ways.

## HEALTHY CONNECTION

How do you establish and maintain deep connectedness and responsible individuality at the same time?

First you recognize your own relationship patterns. You'll need a different perspective to accomplish this. You're too involved in what's "normal," even if it's normal only for you. You may know that you want to have a different type of marriage from the one you were born into, but you may not know how to achieve it. Read a book, see a counselor, seek the input of someone who has cycled further along the course toward a successful marriage. Ask your spouse. He or she can give you a valid, different perspective if you have been building a trusting, honest relationship. Ask your parents or older acquaintances, if there is something in their relationship you'd like to emulate. You won't be able to figure this out on your own.

Lance Armstrong would not be a six-time Tour de France champion without an effective team. He has a conditioning coach to assist him with his training. He has a coach who advises him during the race. He also has teammates and is able to take full advantage of a concept called drafting. In drafting, someone cycles ahead of you, breaking the wind and creating a low resistance area just behind him. You then tuck into that area of decreased resistance. A cyclist can easily reduce his workload by 30 percent or more by drafting.

Draft behind others who can help in your marriage. Take advantage of the wisdom and different perspective of others in order to become a better spouse. Take the initiative to learn from the successes and failures of others. Save your emotional energy for the times when you'll really need it.

Your family of origin is only one group that has shaped you, though its influence is the strongest. You have also been influenced by the social groups, work groups, education groups, racial group, and cultural group to which you belong. All of them have contributed to your attitudes about relationships and marriage.

Admit how at least some of what you learned—maybe your attitudes about yourself and others or various relationship techniques—isn't helping you to move ahead in your marriage. They may even be slowing you down. Travel light. Your development doesn't stop with identifying some deficiencies and admitting that they are hurting your marriage any more than Armstrong's weight loss won him the Tour. They are important first steps, but you still have to do the work. You have to do the work of growth, applying existing skills better or acquiring new skills, knowing that the race will be won in the mountains, where it will be the toughest.

Bonding and separation—the skills may be progressively learned, but they are integrated into your approach to marriage. Two do become one in marriage, but how healthy and strong is the bond? The goal is to be both separate and bonded, two strong individuals living distinct lives as a unified, loving, trusting whole.

Lose the emotional weight; you need to. All of us do. It slows us down. But maintain your strength; you'll need it in the mountains. Keep what works and lose what doesn't. Take advantage of the experiences and wisdom of others. It will make your race easier.

## SUMMARY

"For better or for worse." The phrase is part of the classic marriage vows. It's an acknowledgment that there will be ups and downs. It's not surprising that it also describes our experiences in our families. Whether you were raised by your natural mother and father, a single parent, a parent and a stepparent, or some other person in a parental role, your first lessons about yourself, other people, and relationships were learned in your family. Some of those lessons are bound to be helpful in your marriage, and some are bound to slow you down. You'll have to figure out which is which. Build on those that are helpful. Lose those that slow you down.

## FOR REFLECTION

1.  What two positive relationship patterns from your family of origin do you see yourself using in your own marriage?
2.  What one relationship pattern from your past would you like to stop using in your marriage?

# up where we belong

*It takes time and patience to learn this craft of soaring,*
*but the rewards of moving freely in the air*
*make every moment worthwhile.*

NOEL WHITTALL, paraglider pilot

t all started with an apple, a garden, and a curious mind. You know where this is going, right? Wrong! Different garden. Different apple. Different curious mind. No serpent this time. According to this story, Isaac Newton was having tea in a garden when he saw an apple fall from a tree. He began to question what others took for granted, and before you know it, we had an explanation for something called gravity.

Who knows when man's first thoughts of flight originated? Though it might not have started in exactly this way, some creative, courageous, outside-the-box thinker probably thought, *A bird launches from my roof, flaps its wings a couple of times, and glides. I launch from the roof and straight-line crash into the ground. I'm brighter than the bird but apparently not much different from Newton's apple. What does the bird know that I don't?*

Intuitively the bird understands gliding. The written beginning of man's understanding of gliding appears to be in 1495 when Leonardo da Vinci sketched a crude parachute. Of course the parachute was designed primarily to slow a descent. But there's a big difference between slowing a descent and gliding. Experiments conducted by Francis Rogallo in the 1940s led to the development of hang gliders. In the early 1960s Pierre Lemoigne added slots and cutouts to the classic dome-shaped parachute. The resulting Para Commander parachute, or simply PC, improved the forward speed and control of the chute, giving it some glide performance. In 1964 Domina Jalbert patented the parafoil, a double-surfaced, rectangular canopy with separate sections or cells inflated by air. This new way of managing the airflow was called the "ram air system."

Paragliders emerged from this confluence of technologies. They perform like hang gliders but without the rigid supporting poles and angled kite appearance. They look more like the ram air parachutes, except paragliders are narrower front to back and taper at the outside edges, giving them a more winglike appearance. Whatever their differences, parachutes, hang gliders, and paragliders have one thing in common—they don't defy the law of gravity or any of Newton's laws of motion. In fact, they are remarkably obedient to all of them, especially the earth's tug.

Before embracing paragliding as a hobby, you should be aware of one thing: unless something intervenes, an airborne paraglider is always traveling downward through the air. And he will continue moving downward through the air until something does intervene. That's gravity, and it's the law.

In order to get aloft and stay there, a paraglider pilot has to do one thing: get into air that is moving upward more forcefully than he is moving downward. It's called lift, and a pilot can stumble across it or know how to find it. There are two primary sources of lift.

One place where lift can be found is where a surface-level wind blows steadily against a steep ridge. The air is deflected upward in a broad swath known as a lift band. The best lift bands occur when the wind blows against a ridge that rises steadily, creating a consistent upward flow of air, rather than an abrupt cliff, which results in turbulence. It's also helpful if the wind blows directly into the ridge at a ninety-degree angle. The lift will be strongest near the front of the ridge where the air is suddenly compressed by the ridge. Not surprisingly, this dynamic is known as ridge lift.

Everyone learns to launch their paraglider from a hillside by employing ridge lift. But let's face it, once you've mastered the launch, the basics of flying, and landing, you don't want to spend your paragliding life confined to the relative safety of the launch area. You want to get after it. You want to see what there is to see. You want to, well…spread your wings and fly. You want to go XC, cross-country. You want to go a few miles, and to do that you need to know how to find thermals, the second source of lift.

To understand thermals, it is helpful to remember that the sun does not warm the air. At least not directly. The earth is heated directly by the sun. The surrounding air is warmed by heat radiated back from the surface of the earth. Since the earth is the direct source of heat, it makes sense that the warmest air is that which is nearest to the earth's surface. Warmer air rises and cooler air falls. The earth's surface is not heated evenly. Land heats up and cools off much more quickly than water. A forest is slower to heat up than either a plowed field of rich, dark soil or an asphalt-paved road. It is also slower to cool off.

These variables and more result in a dynamic environment of rising air. For example, the surface of a plowed field that is bracketed by a river on one side and a forest on the other is warmed faster than the surrounding surfaces. Consequently, the air above the field is also warmed faster and eventually begins to rise, creating a thermal. Imagine an enormous, invisible bubble of warm air steadily rising into the sky.

Thermals come in all shapes, sizes, and strengths, depending on the air condition and time of day. As a land-based person, you are no more aware of thermals and lift than you are gravity. You could be standing in a field at 6:00 a.m., completely unaware that you are at the very center of what will become, by noon, a rising mass of air with enough power to keep aloft a paraglider pilot and his forty-five pounds of equipment.

A paraglider pilot who goes XC has learned to identify where the thermals are. When he finds one, he circles within it, quickly gaining altitude with the rising air. And when the thermal breaks up, due to wind and the natural cooling that occurs as air rises, let's say at six thousand feet, he begins his controlled glide downward, searching for the next thermal to start it all over again. This ascend-in-a-thermal and glide-down-to-the-next pattern is repeated over and over again.

"The crux of cross-country flying often lies in correctly answering the question 'Where's the next thermal?' " says Will Gadd. Gadd knows a little about finding thermals. He set a paragliding distance record when he flew 180 miles from Hobbs, New Mexico, to near Bryce, Texas, in 1998. That record was subsequently broken. On June 14, 2002, Gadd arrived in Zapata, Texas, hoping to set another. He flew 150 miles in seven hours on the fifteenth and another 130 miles in a six-hour flight on the nineteenth, a day before a friend established a new record with a 240-mile flight.

Gadd was in the air by 10:00 a.m. on June 21, hoping he could find the strong thermals and consistent wind he'd need for a record try. By 11:00, he'd gone only 20 miles. He caught a strong thermal a half hour later and was quickly lifted to sixty-five hundred feet. By noon, he'd covered another 25 miles. Two hours later he'd gone another 40. It was an enjoyable day doing the thing he loves but not at the pace he'd need to get the record.

He decided to change his strategy and bypass some of the weaker thermals in order to glide farther. Less time climbing meant more time gliding. It made sense, providing he could continue to find strong thermals that would quickly take him higher when he needed to. If he couldn't find them, gravity would see to it that he found the ground, a potentially fatal scenario in this brutally hot, remote, often roadless area of Texas where people attempting to illegally enter the United States often die.

By 3:00 Gadd was 110 miles out. At 3:30 he found himself only four hundred feet off the ground and still descending. At three hundred feet he began to work a light thermal. His light thermal became a "ripper," and he was quickly lifted back up to sixty-five hundred feet as he continued north across the desolate landscape.

Gadd would glide to within a thousand feet of the ground, find the strong thermal he was looking for, and climb back to sixty-five hundred feet. At 6:00 p.m. he'd flown 190 miles. The strategy was working. He was finding the thermals he needed to have a shot at the record. But once again he was on the downward glide in the relentless pull of gravity as he headed for the Texas Hill Country. Thermals are strongest and most frequent in the middle of the day, and Gadd was well beyond midday.

"At about 500 feet above the ground I started to worry; the air had been very still during the glide, a sign that the thermals are shutting down," recalls Gadd. He noticed a group of birds, two hundred feet above the ground, maybe one thousand feet ahead of him. They were climbing well. It would be close, but if he could just stay in the air long enough to reach them, he'd catch what he was sure was his next thermal. And a realistic chance at the record. Stay in the air *and* clear the upcoming power lines. He knew he would either catch the thermal and climb or land while moving dangerously fast.

As he continued his glide down, Gadd felt the glider pressurize and then surge with the thermal. The birds made way for the oversized, wobbly interloper. He cleared the power lines and was carried to nearly six thousand feet in ten minutes. By 7:00 p.m. he was at 220 miles and flying at fifty miles per hour toward where he figured the next thermal was, but he was sinking rapidly. By 7:30 he was back to five hundred feet, trying to determine if the sudden surge of wind and pressure he felt was another thermal that would, once again, take him aloft, or if he had blundered into a violent "rotor" that would likely send him crashing into the wild terrain.

"Something very good or very bad was about to happen," Gadd said. Very good, as it turned out. At 7:45 he was grinning like a man just released from prison. Nearly an hour later he was on the ground, ten hours and thirty-eight minutes and 263 miles from where he began. The record was his again.

Gadd understands Newton. And he willingly accepts the risks of paragliding because the thrill of soaring at six thousand feet is enormously satisfying. But he understands that the thrill and his safety don't just happen. He has to know where to find the thermals and how to position himself so that he soars above the ground rather than crashes into it.

## THE PULL OF CULTURAL GRAVITY

Newton's laws were more universal than he realized. Not only do they explain much of what we experience physically, but they explain much of what we experience mentally and behaviorally.

Think of the world we live in—our culture and the ideas and

behaviors that are considered common and acceptable ("conventional wisdom" let's call it)—as a big gravitational force. We just walk around held firmly in place by a "cultural gravity" that rules our lives, yet it is so pervasive that we never even think about it. Apparently that is not a problem for most people.

But for those who want to soar and experience the incredible satisfaction of an extreme marriage, cultural gravity is an obstacle to overcome, because many of those ideas and behaviors work against a successful marriage. It's not like anyone sets out to have an unsuccessful marriage, but many people are held so firmly in place by cultural gravity that they aren't even aware of the pull.

Just like paragliders, the only way to overcome gravity is to get into air that is moving up more forcefully than gravity is pulling you down. The only air that is moving up more forcefully than cultural gravity is pulling down is the ideal of Christlikeness. First we have to learn about Jesus's character, and the best ways to do so is to actively engage the Bible for yourself by reading it, listening to gifted people teach it, discussing it, and reading books like *Jesus with Dirty Feet*. Those are the thermals in your life. They are the sources of lift you need to keep you aloft. And once you learn about the character of Jesus, you need to recognize how cultural gravity is specifically pulling on you, keeping you stuck on the ground instead of soaring in your marriage.

Hard to believe, but there are actually people who say they believe in the God of Christianity (we're a Christian nation, right?) but think the Bible is outdated in a postmodern society. Silly, huh?

Here's something to consider: regardless of what some people say, biblical wisdom is not a matter of right and wrong. Contrary to what others contend, neither is it a matter of in style or out of style. Biblical wisdom is a type of owner's manual for the establishment and development of healthy, mutually beneficial relationships. The relationship guidelines are as searingly insightful and relevant today as they were thousands of years ago.

Think in terms of constructive or destructive, building up long-term relationships and the people involved or tearing them down. If the Bible says we should do something or not do something, it is not some moral hoop to jump through in order to avoid God's disapproval. It is because that instruction is consistent with how God made us and is in our best interests.

If you want to see how strong the pull of cultural gravity is in your life, take this test: at any point in your day stop and ask yourself, "Is this cultural stimuli—the television show I'm watching, the magazine I'm flipping through, the Web site I'm on, the conversation I'm participating in, the radio program I'm listening to—pointing me toward relating to people as Jesus would or away from that ideal?" No value judgments. No good or bad. Just a simple question. Is the pull toward a Christlike standard or toward something else?

More specifically, at any point in your day stop and ask yourself these questions: "Is what I'm thinking or doing right now strengthening my ability to love and serve my husband or my desire to serve myself?" "If my wife knew what I was thinking or doing right now, would she be inspired to love and serve with greater conviction or be motivated to emotionally protect herself?" "Is what I'm doing or thinking right now building the know-and-be-known companionship in my marriage or raising walls of secrecy and isolation?"

Your answers or your reluctance to answer indicates how deeply entrenched you may be in thinking and behavior patterns that are destructive to your ability to establish and develop long-term, intimate relationships. Your tendency to rationalize your answers with responses like, "But my situation is different because…," "That may have applied two thousand years ago, but today…," or "What the Bible really means…" is an indication of how strong the pull is in your life. Bringing the Bible down to our level is much easier than bringing ourselves up to its level. Watering down the clarity and wisdom of the Bible is a pull.

If you're like many who would take that test, your mind may immediately go to sexual thoughts and behaviors because we live in a sex-saturated culture. Sex sells. Sexual images are used to sell everything from tires to cosmetics. But the most common thing sex sells is dissatisfaction. Images presented in popular media lead us to believe that sex is enjoyed most often and with greatest satisfaction by young, single, physically attractive people who can perform techniques properly. The world is a sexual buffet, but if we're married, not beautiful, or older than forty, we're eating lettuce and carrots.

Those who believe that the unmarried world is a playground of sexual indulgence and satisfaction might find the book *Sex in America: A Definitive Survey* an interesting read. "The usual myths about how easy it is to get new partners and the ways in which youth and beauty translate into frequent partnered sex are false," conclude the authors. Really? But what about those television shows and magazine articles? What about all those jokes about the best way to kill a woman's sex drive is to marry her?

"Those having the most partnered sex and enjoying it the most are married people. The young single people who flit from partner to partner and seem to be having a sex life that is satisfying beyond most people's dreams are, it seems, mostly a media creation. In real life, the unheralded, seldom discussed world of married sex is actually the one that satisfies people the most." The notion that young, attractive, properly proportioned, unmarried people have sex lives that are much more adventurous and satisfying is a gravitational pull.

Beauty, simplicity, the innocence of unmarried sex, and its potential for liberation and maturity—this is the stuff on television twenty-four hours a day. And television has been likened to a sort of national campfire. It provides a place for us to huddle together, warm ourselves, and share a common experience.

National campfire? It is more like a national narcotic. Whether you are an average television viewer (donating about 40 percent of your free time, three to four hours per day) or "only" watch an hour or so a night, most people spend much more time connecting with the television than their spouses and children. Television viewing can be doubly destructive because of the time people devote to it and the general messages it often communicates. The relaxing and recharging qualities attributed to television viewing is a pull.

Do you ever hear something like this on television, in a movie, or in a real conversation? "We've tried, but it's just not working out. Neither one of us is happy. And the kids shouldn't grow up thinking this is what marriage should be like. It's sad, but it will be better for everyone if we cut our losses and move on before any more damage is done."

Or maybe you hear the more hostile version: "I don't know why we ever got married. We have nothing in common. Divorce is the only way out." The underlying premise is the same: though divorce is unfortunate in the general sense, in our case it is better in the long run than an unhappy marriage for both the adults and the children involved.

Many people believe that divorce is the emotional bottoming out. Once the relationship is put behind them, the healing begins. That makes sense. Unfortunately, it overlooks a huge body of contradicting evidence, much of it summarized by Glenn Stanton in his book *Why Marriage Matters.* For instance, divorced men are three times as likely to die—from any cause—than married peers; women are twice as likely. But you don't have to wait to die to pay the price of divorce. The rate of alcoholism is two times higher among divorced adults than those in a stable marriage, three times higher for twice-divorced people. The same ratios hold true for suicide, rates of major depression, and any mental illness. General physical health suffers as well. "Being divorced and a non-smoker is slightly less dangerous than smoking a pack a day and staying married," concludes Harold Morowitz, professor of biophysics at Yale.

Okay, maybe it is hard on the adults, but at least the kids are all right, aren't they? Ever hear that one? Many people believe that kids bounce back relatively quickly after the initial disruption of divorce. But people who grew up in divorced homes often aren't as cheerfully hopeful.

"Divorce carries multiple risks and losses for children, including loss of income, loss of ties with father, loss of residential stability, and loss of other social resources," says Barbara Dafoe Whitehead in *The Divorce Culture.* "The evidence also presented a picture of a downward spiral in children's economic and family fortunes after divorce, with marital dissolution initiating a chain of disruptions and losses. [It] also identified divorce as an important risk factor for school dropout, problem behaviors, lower educational and job achievement, and likelihood of teenage parenthood."

But in the long term the kids are better off, right? They're resilient. They snap back. Sometimes. However, if the work done by Judith Wallerstein, Sandra Blakeslee, and Julia Lewis is accurate, many children who were affected by the divorce of their parents are still suffering the effects as adults. The emotional disruption they experienced as children and the lack of a successful marriage to observe and learn from hinder many adults in their own relationships.

The idea that divorce is an acceptable solution to a challenging marriage, with primarily brief negative consequences to adults and children is a pull.

Most of us don't regard the world as a particularly threatening place to our marriages. So we watch a little television. Maybe we allow our minds to linger over an occasional sexual or emotional fantasy with someone other than our spouse. And what's so bad about divorce (not ours of course) if two people have tried but just can't seem to work things out? It's just the way of the world. It doesn't infect our feelings or undermine our commitment.

Those who feel comfortable in the world and don't feel the constant pull on their marriage might be interested in John Halle's summary of aviation studies comparing accident rates with experience levels. Halle is a former navy pilot and current paraglider pilot. "Just as experience levels reach the point that represents mastery of the environment, accident rates go sharply up!" he says. "This is generally understood to result from a natural tendency to relax one's vigilance once one has concluded that the environment can be mastered and is therefore no longer threatening."

## The Pull of Expectations

All of us have ideas about how the world and relationships work. They are our expectations. We may not be able to say how we acquired our expectations—television or other popular media, the family we grew up in, friends, social institutions—but we have them. And we may not even be able to say what they are. It's usually an unwritten code. Unwritten, but deeply ingrained. What's tricky about our expectations for our spouse and our marriage relationship is that we often aren't aware of what they really are until we are married and our expectations aren't being met. Expectations that are either unreasonable or unidentified can be as troublesome to a successful marriage as the pull of the culture.

Les and Leslie Parrott list four of the most common marriage myths in their book *Saving Your Marriage Before It Starts:*

1. We expect exactly the same things from marriage.
2. Everything good in our relationship will get better.
3. Everything bad in my life will disappear.
4. My spouse will make me whole.

These myths are easy to dismiss as naive when you see them in print. Few people would admit to believing them, but deep within our hearts and minds, most of us cling to one or more.

The reality, of course, is that what each spouse expects from marriage is different. Your expectations of what you should be like as a spouse and what your mate should be like most likely will differ from each other. It's entirely possible to agree in principle on the idea of serving one another in love but disagree on the daily specifics of how that plays out in your marriage. Though hopefully not dramatically different, these different expectations will be sources of tension between the two of you.

Marriage is not a smooth march of positive growth. You will have to fight off equally destructive tendencies of complacency and external distractions to preserve and further develop what is good. The bad that was in your life will still have to be addressed, probably painfully. And though you will likely have strengths and weaknesses that offset and complement each other, you should come to the marriage as nearly whole and complete as possible. The frustration that comes from unreasonable and unidentified expectations not being met is a pull.

Many people believe that a successful marriage is a matter of finding "the one." "The one" who completes you. "The one" God prepared for you. "The one" who makes you happy. "The one" with whom you never fight. "The one" who... Well, don't you just know when he or she is "the one"?

It is true that by making a good spouse choice you can significantly increase your chances for marital satisfaction, decrease disharmony, and free up a great deal of emotional energy for living purposefully. And it is true that a successful marriage needs an intensity, a passionate feeling that your mate is "the one." But it is also true that over the course of your marriage you will encounter enough life and relationship challenges that you may seriously question how you could have possibly been so wrong about his or her being "the one."

"The one" is that person you choose to commit to, not just at the outset of your marriage, but every day. She or he is the one you choose to respect, the one you choose to study and learn about, the one you choose to serve in love, the one you choose to work through difficult issues with, and the one whose needs you choose to put ahead of your own. And that is how the one you fell in love with and married stays "the one" throughout your married life.

A mystical belief that success in marriage means finding "the one" is a pull.

You don't have to look for gravity. Second only to God, gravity is the Great I Am in terms of the power it exerts on us. And here's a big heads up. Because of the strength of our habits, pervasive self-centeredness, and our culture's focus on youth and beauty, the pull of cultural gravity becomes stronger as we age. So you'd better learn how to deal with it now because it will get tougher as you age, much tougher if you don't recognize how strong and destructive the pull is.

Our natural desire is for relationships. We desperately want good ones with spouses, friends, parents, children, work associates—whomever. Unfortunately, our natural tendency is to mess them up. We want them in ways that work best for us, allow us to feel good about ourselves, or don't require more than we are willing to give. We want the benefits of connection without paying the price required for healthy relationships. Our inclination is to crash rather than to soar.

And the tug of the world is strong. It is easier, and short-term safer for many people, to just go along with what we see and what seems to make sense. "There is a way that seems right to a man, but in the end it leads to death," said the writer of Proverbs (14:12).

Incalculable benefits accrue to the wife, the husband, the children, and society as a whole when a man and a woman commit to an emotionally and sexually faithful marriage relationship in which they choose to grow in their understanding of each other and their willingness and ability to serve one another in love. But that is contrary to the force of cultural gravity. Our only chance to overcome that gravitational pull is to get into air that is moving forcefully upward. And the only air that is safe, consistent, and powerful enough to keep us up is Christlikeness.

## SUMMARY

If we fail to see the incredible possibilities of an extreme marriage, we will most likely fail to understand how purposeful we have to be in its pursuit. Overt threats like unfaithfulness are a danger to all marriages. But for most of us, it's the hundred little distractions of everyday life—the sloppy thinking, the rationalized indulgences, the relational laziness, the failure to make a successful marriage a high priority—that tug at us and rob us of the energy we need to invest in our marriages. We stay stuck on the ground, either complacent or frustrated, instead of seeking out the thermals and soaring.

## FOR REFLECTION

1. What one Bible verse is most important to you in how you approach each day of your marriage?

2. When thinking of the specific distractions you encounter, what does that verse challenge you to do?

3. Would you be willing to ask your spouse (and listen to his or her response) which distraction he or she thinks has the strongest pull on you?

# The Trail Less Traveled

## Expressing Love to a Spouse Is Like Mountain Biking

*What constitutes a "good" mountain biking trail?*
*It's anything that's fun to ride....*
*The state of being that is fun comes from an acceptance,*
*an embracing of the process.*
*You can't have fun with something when you're fighting it*
*or wishing it were somehow different.*

DAVE KING AND MICHAEL KAMINER, mountain bikers

Just like riding a bike, once you learn how, you never forget."
The memories of learning to ride a bike are often our first memories of a true learning experience. Our parents might have very special memories of our first awkward attempts at walking and talking, but we don't. Those base-level skills were established before we even realized they were learned. As far as we knew, we were natural-born walkers and talkers.

But bicycling was learned. It was an effort we made, and we knew it. What we didn't know was how life changing it would be.

It offered the promise of freedom and discovery. It gave us a means to escape the watchful eyes of our parents before we even realized it was escape we would someday want. It allowed us to explore new neighborhoods, visit friends' houses, and get to fun playgrounds. Once we got the balance and pedaling things figured out, it seemed like riding a bike was the most natural thing in the world, and life would never be the same.

Maybe you're one of those people who learned to ride a bike on the quiet paved street you grew up on. That would be natural, since biking is initially a complex activity with a potentially painful learning curve. Adult assistance, training wheels, paved surfaces—best to minimize the variables, and pain, while you acquire balance and basic skills. But eventually what was a challenge became second nature. You could go as far and as fast as your little legs, and maybe your parents' rules, would allow. One day you came to a fork of sorts. The smooth, paved road upon which you had been easily pedaling curved gently to the right and up another gradual hill. But to the left you noticed a little-used trail that dipped quickly down an embankment and ducked mysteriously into the woods. What to do? To go with what you know or to take a chance on what you don't?

Well, of course, just like Robert Frost, you "took the one less traveled by, and that has made all the difference." And when you went off-road, you quickly discovered that though pedaling and balance were still critical, you'd have to acquire a whole new set of skills to enjoy this trail less traveled. You had entered the realm of mountain biking, and once again your world would never be the same.

Maybe you're one of those people whose body tenses as effort increases. That would make sense, especially as you climb. As fatigue builds and your ability to respond quickly to changes diminishes, you need to be particularly vigilant to maintain control. Ironically, as effort and fatigue increase, what you need to be vigilant about is relaxing.

Sometimes it is most helpful to do what feels least natural. Relax your grip on the handlebars. A tight grip results in excessive muscle tension in your hands, forearms, neck, and shoulders. If you focus on relaxing your hands and jaw, the rest of your body will follow. A relaxed upper body not only saves energy, it also absorbs jolts better and gives you more control in the technical sections.

"Tense mountain bikers ride like ice cubes. They bounce down a trail instead of flowing over it. Every shock from the ground is transmitted from the bike through their still limbs. Their steering is unpredictable. They fatigue quickly. They lack stability and control. They are uncomfortable." Not exactly a list of must-haves for a positive mountain biking experience.

Maybe you're one of those people who take great gasping breaths when engaged in strenuous activity. Deep on the inhale, shallow on the exhale. Most of us do, since breathing is a survival instinct, and when your system is distressed, great sucking gasps make the most sense.

Good mountain bikers know the importance of breathing that is smooth rather than gasping. When gasping, we naturally quicken our breathing to a deep-inhale, shallow-exhale pattern. If you learn to focus on exhaling with force, the inhale part will take care of itself. Your breaths will be full and deep rather than shallow and inefficient. Breathe like a machine, and learn to synchronize your breaths with your pedal strokes. That will help you develop an efficiently coordinated rhythm of breathing and pedaling.

Maybe you're one of those people who fix their gaze just in front of the bike's front wheel. That would be natural since it's the obstacles and irregularities that are closest to you that present the greatest immediate threat to your balance and general well-being.

Good mountain bikers are good readers of the trail that is in front of them. Not immediately in front of them, because they read that awhile back. They read the trail that is maybe thirty to forty feet out. Mountain bikers call it the "line." The line is simply the path you choose to get through a section of your ride, a sort of trail within the trail. There are good lines, "the ones that keep your bike moving the fastest with the least amount of energy expended," and there are bad lines that make you work harder than you have to or unnecessarily expose you to danger.

Reading a line is a matter of seeing what is before you well before it is right before you. That way you can anticipate the terrain and avoid the sudden stops, starts, and turns that can make mountain biking more frustrating and painful than exciting. When you combine this sort of vision with judgment, the quick ability to know what skills are required and whether or not you can confidently execute them, you'll achieve the off-roaders' Zen-like level of "flowing like water."

The more challenging the trail, the greater the need for a good line. On some trails, "it's the good line or no line, the perfect line or the painful limp." Sounds like a good skill to have. The best readers scan the terrain in a continual visual sweep of the trail, from as far ahead as they can see to the back in front of their wheel. They concentrate on keeping the line rather than avoiding the obstacles.

Maybe you're one of those people who hit the brakes hard just before or after an obstacle or a particularly challenging section. That seems like the right thing to do, because you'd want to feel most in control just before you need to be most in control. The problem is that braking reduces, not increases, control. "A rotating front wheel is more likely to roll through a tricky section than one clamped between brake pads. A rotating front wheel won't dig into the ground after a drop-off or a downhill log jump. A rotating front wheel pulls you through a switchback. It leads the bike across loose scut instead of demanding to be pushed. It finds ways over hub-high rocks."

Maybe you're one of those people who try to break their fall by stretching out their arms, hands, and fingers. That would make sense, because the idea of crashing headfirst or shoulderfirst into the ground seems like a dangerous choice. However, by stretching out your arms, hands, and fingers, you're as likely to break them as you are your fall. Falling is an integral part of mountain biking, just another variable in the risk-reward equation. So if you want to spend more time cycling than healing, it's best to learn how to fall correctly.

Keep your arms and hands in. Roll when possible. It dissipates the force of the impact more gradually and across a wider surface area of your body. If you're sure there are no sudden drop-offs or imminent hazards, stop as quickly as reasonably possible. If you're starting to crash on a descent, you may be able to simply step off your bike and run to a stop while it continues on without you—just like the bull riders in the rodeos.

Believe it or not, experts say that if you get launched forward, it's often best to hang on to the handlebars and stay clicked in to your pedals. It seems that the sturdy bike frame, which is built to absorb impact, continues to absorb impact pretty well even in the chaos of a fall. But it's an all-or-nothing deal. You have to both hang on and stay clicked in so you and the bike are one tumbling mass. If you hang on but click out of your pedals, you could become a violently twisting, intertwining mass.

"Your riding experience will at first feel like an epic battle between you and your intuition," warns Dave King in *The Mountain Bike Experience.* "Wipe the slate clean. Unlearn your intuition on the trail…. With experience, you learn to rethink. And you find the harmony that's halfway between freedom and fear." What was once ignorance becomes an awkward learning curve. But you do it because the promise of off-road adventure is stronger than your discomfort or fear. And soon your learning curve will become second nature. Once you have the skills, not only can you take the trail less traveled, you can enjoy the experience. You're no longer thinking about how to ride. You're riding and having a blast!

## Marriage—A New Trail, Some New Skills

Whether you knew it or not, when you came to that fork in your road and decided, not just to marry, but to pursue an extreme marriage, you chose the trail less traveled, and it will make all the difference. Hopefully the base-level relationship skills that you developed as a single are solid. But once you got married, a whole new skill set was necessary to love your spouse, at least to express your love to him or her in understandable ways.

Understanding how to tell someone that he or she is loved is different from simply saying, "I love you." The words we say and hear are only part of the process. Communication occurs on many levels. Gary Chapman has identified five ways that people understand that they are loved. He calls them love languages. They are as real as any spoken language. Of all the things that Tari and I have learned about how to have a thriving marriage, understanding and applying Chapman's love-language concepts have had the single biggest impact.

A love language is like hearing or saying, "I love you," without those actual words being said. All of us have at least one primary love language, whether we can identify it or not. Unfortunately, we tend to choose spouses who don't have the same love language. Consequently, regardless of how sincere or skilled we are at expressing love in the ways that feel most comfortable and natural, unless our spouse has that same language, it will be a mutually frustrating experience.

When our spouse "speaks" our language, we feel loved. But the reverse is true as well. When our spouse doesn't speak it, we don't feel loved. We may see the evidence of love, and we may recognize it on an intellectual level, but we don't feel loved at a deep soul level.

Don't panic. Think of love languages as a relationship skill set, much like climbing and descending hills are skill sets for mountain biking. They can be learned. Once you learn your spouse's love language and develop the habit of regularly speaking it, the more satisfying the experience will be for both of you. We learned this about love languages while still dating. We also learned that our languages were different. That explained why the acts of service (my language) I performed for her didn't touch her as I'd hoped. It also explains why the words of affirmation (her language) she so generously spoke to me didn't move me as she expected. Not surprisingly, when we began to consistently speak each other's language, we turned a significant corner in our relationship.

## THE LOVE LANGUAGES

The first love language Chapman identifies in his book *The Five Languages of Love* is *words of affirmation*. Words of affirmation are those that build up, are kind or encouraging. They affirm the value of your spouse. These words let your mate know that he or she is important. Words that communicate "I notice you, I respect you, I love you" are powerful for all people, but especially for those who have words of affirmation as their primary love language.

An obvious but often overlooked condition of expressing love in this way is that first you have to notice something about your partner or something he or she is doing. In the swirl of life, it can be easy to overlook positive qualities of your mate. As the routine of living together becomes established, attributes that once stood out in your mind now blend into the landscape of your relationship. And even if you do notice, it can also be easy to overlook the verbal part, the part that lets him or her know that you appreciate the fact that she keeps herself in good shape, that you value his insights, that he is a great partner in parenting, or that you value how reliable she is.

I know about this one firsthand. I can't tell you how many times I've noticed something positive about Tari—how nice she looks in a new outfit when we're going out, for instance—and failed to say the words. I have a small, flat spot on my forehead from smacking it after she asks me if I like what she's wearing. I've blown a chance to let her know in a way that is especially meaningful to her that I notice her and am attracted to her. And I wish I could tell you it's as trivial as simply not commenting on what she's wearing, but sometimes it's more significant. There have been times when I've failed to encourage her in an area she's growing in or failed to acknowledge something meaningful she's accomplished.

The second love language is *quality time.* Chapman says that quality time has a lot to do with togetherness. Togetherness is about focused attention not proximity. Talking with each other, listening to each other, keeping abreast of each other's world is a necessary component of any successful marriage, especially as other responsibilities compete for your emotional energy. People with quality time as a primary love language do not regard sharing time and conversation as a strategy to keep their marriage on track. It is a need in order for them to flourish as a person.

Sharing activities is one expression of quality time. Your spouse doesn't have to have your complete and undivided attention as long as you're sharing a meaningful activity. Time together is the focus, not the activity itself. And it doesn't have to be an elaborate or expensive activity. Going to the zoo, taking a walk, taking the kids to the park together are all examples of shared activities. Another night in couch-potato position, remote in hand, is probably not a meaningful shared activity.

Since conversation is probably part of time together, Chapman offers some conversation habits that both keep you in the conversation and communicate interest. Don't multitask. Focus on your spouse by maintaining eye contact and observing body language. Listen for feelings and refuse to interrupt. Seek to understand.

*Receiving gifts* is Chapman's third language of love. As with the other four, you may need to expand your definition of *gifts* to grasp Chapman's point. Gifts can be found, purchased, or made. They can be tangible, like a new watch, or intangible, like taking the kids so your spouse can enjoy dinner with an old friend or a round of golf after a tough week. They can be expensive, like a new leather coat, or inexpensive, like a single rose. One thing they always are to the person whose primary love language is gifts—thoughtful.

What you verbalize when you give a gift is something like, "Here, this is for you. I love you." What you communicate is, "I care enough to have learned that gifts are important to you. We're connected enough that I know what's going on in your life and what kinds of things you value. I'm committed enough to take the time to get this for you. I love you."

*Acts of service* are Chapman's fourth love language. When you do things for your spouse that make his or her life somehow better or easier, you're speaking your spouse's language of love. People who don't have this language don't understand how doing housework, stopping by the store to pick up light bulbs, or taking the car in for an oil change communicates heartfelt love. But people who do have this language understand. And that's a key to love languages. You don't have to get it to do it. Knowing that it is important to your spouse is all you need to know. To do the work, you don't need to understand why it works.

*Physical touch* is Chapman's final love language. And many men will say, "That's mine. When we're making love is when I feel most loved by and most in love with my wife." It's true that making love is a powerful aspect of a relationship, but it's probably not as important as other, more mundane expressions to the person whose primary love language is physical touch.

Holding hands when you walk together, reassuringly squeezing your husband's shoulder as you walk past, and hugging your wife when you leave each other in the morning or reconvene at night are certainly more frequent physical expressions. When added together, all those little touches are probably more significant than making love to the person who has this language.

"If your spouse's primary love language is physical touch, nothing is more important than holding her as she cries," offers Chapman as a special heads up to men. Holding a woman while she cries—now there's a learned skill for most men and apparently an important one. There's something both healing and sealing about making the effort to speak your spouse's love language after conflict or in a time of crisis. When one of you has been hurt or a situation has threatened the connectedness of your relationship, it's critical to express your support and commitment to your spouse. Even if the conflict is not resolved or the crisis has not passed, your commitment remains absolutely unshaken. Speaking your spouse's language at these times serves the equally important functions of reassuring him or her and refocusing yourself.

In mountain biking, it's natural to brake before steep descents or when encountering a challenging section. Remember that a smoothly rotating wheel has more stability than one that is clamped between brake pads. In times of conflict or stress in your life or marriage, it's natural that your concern for your own well-being will rise. It's easy to fall back into a "But what about me?" focus. These are the times you may feel least like expressing love and reassurance to your spouse. You will be tempted to hit the relational brakes. Don't do it. Keep pedaling toward connection.

It's most important to be loving and reassuring when you least feel like it. It helps you drive another nail into the coffin of self-orientation and entitlement rather than a wedge into your relationship. And though that's true of any of the languages, it's probably most true of physical touch. Whether it's a hug or a gift or a sincere "I love you," speaking your spouse's language isn't a substitute for the hard work of conflict management. It's a final step that binds you back together.

## LEARNING TO SPEAK THE LANGUAGES FLUENTLY

Like all the other relationship skills, speaking our spouses' love languages is a matter of ongoing skill development. Even after we know them and have a base-level competency in speaking them, new circumstances will continually reveal refinements that we'll need to make as life moves on, just as new biking trails challenge us to grow.

If we want to improve as spouses, we need to solicit the input of our mates. They need to coach us on how to better meet their needs. This is true in learning the language in the first place but especially true in refining our expressions to hit the target dead-on. Learning to speak a language may represent skill development for you. Congratulations on taking a significant step! But just like mountain biking, if you want to continue enjoying your sport, you need to improve those skills.

Likewise, our spouses will need our input to improve. In order for us to help them grow and become better mates, we have to know ourselves. Back to that self-discovery thing we were supposed to have taken care of a long time ago. Many people don't know what their love language is or that the concept even exists. That's okay; you can figure it out.

Pay attention to what your spouse says or does, or fails to say or do, that hurts you deeply. For example, do you find yourself yearning for an expression of respect that never comes? Words of affirmation could be your language. Pain can be a valuable tool in the learning process. You can also think of what you have most often requested of your mate. Do you ask him or her to help you get things done? Acts of service might be it for you. Of course, you can flip this process and study your spouse to determine what she is asking for, how he responds to nonsexual touch, or what things you might have said or done that seemed to lift her spirits or to discourage him. These would all be clues to each other's love languages.

Perhaps the most reliable clue of your language is the one you naturally speak to your spouse. Do you make a mental note of things she notices and later give them to her as gifts? Your language is likely gifts. Do you just like hanging out, spending time with him? Time is probably your language. Do you naturally see things that you could help with and do them? If so, acts of service done for you are most likely the clearest way you feel loved. We are all most likely to speak the language we know best.

Since they are triply beneficial, love languages are an extremely efficient skill to master. First of all, the fact that you even learned them and identified your spouse's language demonstrates a commitment to growth in your marriage that many people never make. Second, when you speak your spouse's language, he or she feels loved at the deepest level. And third, because your spouse's language is most likely different from yours, speaking his or her love language will always be a loving act of your will or a positive habit that you've chosen to develop. It keeps you focused on your spouse's needs instead of your own. One concept, three benefits.

Just like riding a bike, once you learn how, you never forget. With practice and the trail wisdom that comes only with riding, the skills of mountain biking can become as natural as the balancing and pedaling you learned as a kid. And the more second nature they become, the more satisfying your adventure will be.

Marriage is an adventurous trail we choose to ride. Hills and gullies, rocks and streams, roots and logs—you'll encounter them all on the marriage trail. Regardless of how solid you are on the road, don't assume you'll make it if you don't have the skills of the trail.

## Summary

Your marriage relationship is a new adventure. To maximize your satisfaction and your spouse's, you'll have to learn what love language each of you has. And after you determine what they are, you'll have to develop the habit of speaking your spouse's language.

## FOR REFLECTION

1.  What is your spouse's primary love language?
2.  What specific things could you do to speak it?
3.  What is your love language?

# If it were easy, everybody would be doing it

## Conflict management is like a triathlon

> *It all begins with a simple goal:*
> *to swim, bike, and run your way from a starting line*
> *to a finish line as fast as you are able.*
> MATT FITZGERALD, triathlete

It's an unnatural act, plain and simple. An unnatural act made up of unnatural acts. The unnatural whole is greater than the sum of its unnatural parts. An unnatural act performed by...well, let's be kind here, performed by unusually purposeful people who are unusually committed to an unusual goal, and that's not so natural either. Let's give them a name. How about triathletes?

How natural is it to swim 2.4 miles? Few people on the planet have ever done it. And how natural is it to ride a bicycle 112 miles? Maybe a few more people have done it, but it's not a natural activity. And how natural is running 26.2 miles? Most people alive today probably haven't run 26.2 miles over the course of their entire lives. To do all three over a period of twelve or thirteen hours? An unnatural act, don't you agree?

Like many extreme sports, the origin of the triathlon is difficult to precisely determine. Most likely it was a group of fitness specialists whose judgment was emboldened by endorphins or clouded by alcohol, looking for activities that would still give them the benefits of training without the monotony. It is generally agreed that Hawaii is the official headwaters of formal triathlons. Some locals came up with the crazy notion of combining the three Oahu endurance events—the Waikiki Rough Water Swim, the Around Oahu Bike Ride, and the Honolulu Marathon—into one event with the grandiose name of the Ironman. The first was run in 1978, and each year a few more athletes decided to compete. The sport rocketed into the public's awareness in 1982 when Ironman competitor Julie Moss was shown crawling across the finish line on ABC's *Wide World of Sports*. The sport gained instant recognition and its participants a reputation as unbalanced zealots.

Triathlons begin with an open-water swim because, well, if you ended with the swim, DNF would be the acronym for Drowned, Never Found instead of Did Not Finish. Swimming is a barrier for many athletes who might otherwise compete. It is the discipline in which the most number of people have the least amount of experience. It is also the most difficult event for which to train. You can pull on running shoes, step outside your door, and be on a training run in no time. Same thing with a bicycle. Not swimming. Most training is done in pools—temperature controlled to keep you comfortable, floating lane dividers to minimize waves and keep you on track, lines on the bottom of the pool to guide you, and every twenty-five meters a break in your stroking while you turn at the wall.

An open-water swim has none of those conveniences. You're at the mercy of weather and waves. No walls means no breaks while you turn. There is nothing to guide you but the buoys that mark the course. And the only way to get from one buoy to another is to keep sighting them while you stroke, something even competitive swimmers usually haven't learned to do. So every eighth stroke is a strong "Tarzan" stroke in which you pull yourself up, arch your neck to bring your head out of the water, and find the buoy.

The start of the swim, which is also the start of the entire race, is unlike any other part. The swim leg is an endurance event, like all the others, but it begins with a crowded sprint to the water. Once in the water it's a shoulder-to-shoulder, feet-to-face exercise in courteous (sometimes) and controlled (usually) violence in which noses sometimes get broken. It's more like a mass of wriggling tadpoles than a wave of highly conditioned athletes.

Just about anybody can swim, if swimming means getting from one end of the pool to the other without drowning. But completing a 2.4-mile course in open water with enough energy left for the cycling and running stages is entirely different.

At the conclusion of the swimming section, you'll be approaching T1, the transition area from swimming to biking. The two transitions in triathlons (biking to running being the second and typically harder of the two) have been called the fourth event. The goal is to get through them as quickly as possible, and to do so you need to move deliberately and efficiently rather than hastily. It's a good idea to spend the last couple of minutes of each event mentally reviewing and rehearsing the upcoming transition—how you've organized your bag, where your gear is located, what the sequence is. Being organized and having the routine down are critical because fatigue has a way of scrambling your thinking.

Smooth, efficient, purposeful. On to the next event.

After swimming comes cycling. Cycling accounts for about 50 percent of a triathlete's finish time. It's the best area to be strong in and the worst area to be weak in. In training, it offers the most room for improvement. It also offers the most opportunity to gain time during the race. But a rider must also exercise race wisdom by not going too fast. In the early part of a race, maybe the first ten or eleven hours, triathletes must always factor how their current efforts will affect performance near the end.

An Ironman distance triathlon means you're strenuously exerting yourself for around thirteen hours, maybe more, maybe less, depending on your natural abilities and level of fitness. Staying properly hydrated and fed is essential for effective performance. The cycling leg is the best place to ensure that your body has what it needs. It's kind of tough to eat or drink when you're stroking through a lake. Many triathletes find that as the race progresses and more and more energy is expended, their motivation to eat diminishes. Experienced racers know that regardless of whether they feel like it, eating and drinking are as much a part of triathlon success as swimming, cycling, and running.

"Twenty miles of hope and six miles of reality," is how Ironman champion Cameron Brown describes the final event, a full-length marathon. Triathlon running is unlike other running races because the athlete, having just completed a swim of more than an hour and cycled for six hours or longer, runs in a fatigued state. The first mile will be hard as your body adjusts to the new motion, but eventually you'll feel better. "Feel better" is relative. You'll never feel *good*, and at some point you will hit the wall.

"The race really begins somewhere near the end of the first half of the marathon," say Joe Friel and Gordon Byrn in their book *Going Long: Training for Ironman Distance Triathlons.* That's when you find out if your training has given you the physical resources to continue what you started and whether you have the resolve to finish.

The area of training and performance that lags furthest behind all the others is not physical, but mental. A triathlete's mind has to be in as good a shape as his body if he wants to finish, better if he wants to excel. At those times of doubt, discomfort, and fatigue, the ultimate goal and its benefits must be firmly fixed in your heart and mind. "If we cannot master our emotions, we cannot minimize negative emotions, which waste energy and cause us to perform beneath our true potential," warns triathlete Matt Fitzgerald. "At the root, there is only one negative emotion: fear. The self-doubt that overtakes us just before the race starts, the urge to quit that gains sway when the race becomes painful, the brooding we do when we experience a setback in training—these emotions are all forms of fear, and all counterproductive in relation to our desire to achieve success as triathletes."

Balance is the key to being a successful triathlete. Balance, as in managing your expectations through all events, expecting to pass others and to be passed by others, expecting the pain and discomfort, even expecting the unexpected. Balance, as in knowing the difference between the pain that comes with extreme exertion and the pain that warns of long-term injury. Balance, as in pacing, expending energy as efficiently as possible over the course of these three separate tests of endurance. Balance, as in being proficient in these three different skills.

"Those with backgrounds in all three have the best chance of holding their position. That's the solution to winning in this sport—balance," says veteran triathlete Sally Edwards.

## The Triathlon of Conflict in Marriage

Extreme marriage has its own three-discipline event. Conflict management is the event, and it is made up of the three different skills of *conflict resolution, living with "perpetual problems,"* and *forgiveness.* It is an event you must win to have a marriage that not only will last a lifetime but will become increasingly rewarding as you go through life together. And to win, you have to become proficient in all three events.

The word *conflict* has picked up a bad rap over the years. For many people the word means an argument or an angry outburst. For others it is a vague sense that things aren't as they should be or the work of the relationship is harder than they expected. For these people, to experience conflict in a relationship means that something bad is happening. Those who believe in the myth of "the one" may conclude that they have made, or are making, a bad choice. Because there is conflict, this person is not "the one."

Marital conflict is simply the disharmony that results when expectations aren't met. It can result from something as small as leaving the cap off the toothpaste or as significant as how and how often you make love. Conflict can be obvious, like how much time to spend in life-maintenance activities like cleaning the home, or hidden, like dealing with the residue of growing up as a child of an alcoholic parent.

Conflict is the natural and inevitable result of two becoming one. Two people, a man and a woman, different from each other physically, psychologically, emotionally, and sexually, decide they want to marry. Those innate differences will be multiplied by differences in their families of origin, education, friendships, business experiences, and much, much more. Now compound those differences even further by the fact that we tend to choose partners who are at least somewhat different from us. The final multiplier in the conflict formula is our own self-centeredness, our desire to have relationships on our terms. Multiplied together, the innumerable combinations of these variables can result in significant differences and potential sources of conflict.

"A couple's ability to deal with differences is a sign of maturity," say Henry Cloud and John Townsend. You are different from each other, and regardless of how much genuine effort you invested in the discovery of yourselves and each other, those differences will be magnified in marriage. And many others will be discovered for the first time.

Conflict is a way of life. And if you don't have a good understanding of conflict management and its components of conflict resolution, living with perpetual problems, and forgiveness, conflict may also be a way of relational death. It is up to you.

"Make conflict your ally, not your enemy," advise Cloud and Townsend. "It is the iron that sharpens your marriage." It can be the tool that you use to grow as individuals and as a couple, or it can be the weapon you each use to defend yourselves, hurt your spouse, and damage your marriage. As a tool, it can help you uncover hidden issues—your own and those of your spouse.

Money, sex, communication, family and friends of one partner or the other, and how you spend your time are all common and understandable sources of conflict. However, it's also common that these issues are merely triggers for what the authors of *Fighting for Your Marriage* call hidden issues.

Hidden issues are often at the root of the most intense, frequent, unproductive, and damaging discussions. Hidden issues are often driven by previous relationships in which there was betrayal, abuse, or deeply felt but chronically unmet needs. The person's expectations and even sense of self were seriously violated.

*Control* is the first of the hidden issues. Who's in charge? Who makes the decisions? Is the power shared equally, or does it belong disproportionately to one partner?

*Recognition,* another hidden issue, revolves around "feeling valued by your partner for who you are and what you do." It's a matter of feeling appreciated.

*Feeling cared for* is another hidden issue. If your most important emotional needs are not being met, you won't feel cared for and loved.

*Integrity,* the fourth hidden issue, has to do with one partner questioning the intentions and motives of the other. Regardless of what the true motive may be, what does one partner believe about why the other does what he or she does?

*Commitment* issues involve "the long-term security of the relationship, expressed by the question 'Are you going to stay with me?'"

And "the mother of all issues"? *Acceptance.* "At the deepest level, people are motivated to find acceptance and avoid rejection in their relationships." Many surface-level conflicts are really expressions of these five obscured issues. And many of these hidden issues stem from an unmet need for acceptance. Acceptance is an essential part of the foundation of any marriage. You cannot build a successful marriage on a foundation that is cracked and crumbling due to a lack of acceptance.

Hidden issues can exert a pervasive influence on your relationship. They have the potential to touch all aspects of how you relate to each other. This is especially true in times of conflict, when extremely sensitive emotional areas can be poked in a setting of hurt, frustration, and disappointment.

## Resolving Conflict

Research conducted by marriage expert John Gottman led him to conclude that conflicts fall into two categories: solvable and perpetual. Solvable conflicts can be resolved if the individuals care enough to develop the skills and to go through the process.

So what is the conflict-resolution process? The first is obvious—you have to recognize that one or both of you has unmet expectations. And once you recognize the situation, someone has to initiate a discussion about it.

In most relationships, that will be the wife more often than the husband. Generally speaking, women are more sensitive to what's going on in the relationship and are more accurate in their perceptions. Also, because of apparently natural gender predisposition and social training, women are more comfortable, or at least less uncomfortable, verbalizing their feelings and observations and working out a solution.

"If there is one similarity between happy and unhappy marriages, it's that in both circumstances the wife is far more likely than the husband to bring up a touchy issue and to push to resolve it," says Gottman. Certainly that pattern is not always the case. As a matter of fact, if a man believes he has a leadership role and takes it seriously, he shouldn't depend on his wife to acknowledge issues and initiate discussions. If he is learning to live with his wife in an understanding way, he is also learning to identify developing concerns. By sharing that responsibility, a husband demonstrates that he is fully committed to what the relationship is now and what it can become.

Regardless of whether the man or woman initiates the discussion, what Gottman calls a "soft start-up" is essential. It is based on a widely accepted principle of human relations that interactions almost always end the way they begin. If you want to come out of a discussion about some area of conflict with clarified expectations, greater knowledge of your spouse and yourself, an affirmed respect for each other, an unshaken commitment to the marriage team, and a renewed sense that you share the ultimate goal of becoming more like Jesus, go into the discussion with that in mind and act accordingly.

If you don't want your discussion to end that way, then just let it fly. Do what comes naturally. Just win, baby. Control, short-term false peace, image management, protection of some little idol of indulgent behavior—whatever is important to you, just do it.

In triathlons, you decide what you're committed to before the pain and discomfort come. It's the same thing in conflict resolution. Decide what you're moving toward in your marriage before you're faced with the negative emotions of unmet expectations.

If you want positive results, here's some soft start-up advice. Statements that begin with "I" and describe what is happening or how the situation makes you feel will be much more effective than statements that begin with "you." We've all been there—the tense, accusatory words that find fault, fix blame, or judge motive or character. It's okay to complain about a specific situation, but it's not okay to accuse your partner or blame him or her for the problem. Be clear about the issue, appreciative of any positive steps previously taken, and genuinely polite and respectful.

As you talk, be thorough about identifying the issue. You're not judging; you're discovering. Clearly identify the issue before you even think of ways to solve it. Try as hard to understand your partner's thoughts and feelings as you do to make him or her understand yours. Conflict is rarely a matter of one partner being all right and one being all wrong. We all contribute in various ways to the imperfections in our marriages. Though we may contribute less to one issue, we probably contribute somehow. And most likely we will make up for it by being disproportionately "generous" in our contribution to another. Be willing to compromise if compromise moves the relationship ahead, is not part of a larger pattern of compliance or manipulation, and does not violate important principles.

Setting time expectations on resolution of a conflict is important. Because of the emotional nature of unmet expectations, it can be a challenge to engage in a productive discussion at the moment when the conflict is painfully experienced. Acknowledging the issue but setting up a better time to talk about it demonstrates good judgment and commitment to the relationship, if you keep the commitment and revisit the issue. Generally, the longer the discussion, the more vulnerable it becomes to someone losing patience or a partner less skilled in conflict resolution making some kind of mistake. The process can head south pretty quickly. Triathlons are not the only place where pain and fatigue can scramble your thinking.

Own what is yours to own—your contribution to the problem, your feelings of hurt or disappointment, your need to apologize, your need to accept an apology, and more—but only what is yours. Keep on track. One issue at a time, please. Don't drag in other things you're unhappy about. Learn to monitor yourself and your spouse for signs that, in the midst of the demanding event of conflict resolution, you're getting scared or losing sight of a productive endpoint.

You know you're getting lost or scared when someone starts escalating the discussion through tone of voice or accusation, putting the other person down through words or gestures, withdrawing emotionally or physically, or projecting negative motives onto the partner. If you observe those signs in yourself or your partner, it's time to stop. Call time-out and calm yourselves instead of continuing to flail away in hurt or frustration. Remind yourselves of where you're headed, or at least where you said you were headed. If the relationship doesn't win, you both lose in the long term.

Inexperienced triathletes make two common mistakes in the transition areas. First, they try to race through them. They underestimate how much their body has adjusted to performing one skill for so long or how disoriented they might be from fatigue. They awkwardly stumble three or four times trying to put on their shoes as they transition from swimming to cycling, for example. They end up losing rather than gaining time. Or they may linger too long, understandably enjoying the break in the exertion. But the longer a racer stays in the transition area, piddling around with equipment and talking to race volunteers, the more difficult it can be to get going again.

People inexperienced at healthy conflict resolution often make the same two mistakes. Some people race through conflict discussions, if they have them at all, because of their discomfort in conflict and fear of how it could negatively affect themselves and the relationship. Getting back to something that feels more like peace, even if it's false or short-term, is their goal, rather than real progress toward a mutually beneficial resolution.

Others linger in the conflict. They don't want to arrive at a mutually beneficial endpoint. Maybe they want to punish the other person with either cold silence or damaging words. Maybe they want to punish themselves. Regardless of who they want to punish, moving the relationship ahead requires growth, something many people are much more eager to see in their mate than pursue in themselves.

## LIVING WITH PERPETUAL PROBLEMS

The second type of conflict referred to by Gottman—perpetual conflict—is the kind that couples talk about, probably even argue over, again and again and again. This year's conflicts will likely be next year's conflicts, which will likely be the same conflict five years from now. They don't get resolved.

Gottman estimates that 69 percent of a couple's conflicts are perpetual. Couples who have learned… Wait a minute! If you didn't stop to reread that last sentence, the 69 percent sentence, you need to. Thorough research conducted by one of the country's leading marriage experts leads him to the conclusion that 69 percent of a couple's conflicts will most likely be a part of their relationship for the rest of their lives. Sixty-nine percent! Almost *seven* out of *ten*!

Successful marriages aren't the ones that don't have perpetual conflicts. All marriages do. Successful marriages are the ones in which the husband and wife understand that problems are part of relationships. They also don't let their differences, and the issues that result, overwhelm their positive feelings for each other. They have found, probably through painful lessons of trial and error, how to dialogue without yielding to hopelessness or wielding demands for change. Because they are neither hopeless nor demanding, honest dialogue keeps their hearts from becoming hard.

"The rub" is what Steve and Valerie Bell use to describe perpetual problems in their book *Made to Be Loved*. The rub is "that which is innately different and mostly unchangeable about each other." It's relational friction. It's what happens when a morning person marries an evening person. It's what happens when one partner, once again, insists on staying at the party that the other partner, once again, never wanted to go to in the first place. It's what happens when one partner makes decisions based on his gut feeling and the other methodically gathers information and carefully deliberates. The residue of these differences builds over the years. What once might have been endearing differences become annoyances. And what were annoyances might increasingly become all we notice when we think about or interact with our spouse.

"Left unaddressed, the rub can become the obsessional focus of a marriage relationship. 'Change' we demand of each other. 'Change so I can easily love you again.' We wrestle each other's egos to the ground and demand reform, demand readjustment, demand compatibility. Hostility increases when change is slow or does not happen at all."

The Bells offer a three-step process called "smoothing the rub." The first step is obvious and something many couples have already done—identify the rub. The second step—accepting the rub—is a little harder. That will involve changing our perspective, which we can do, rather than changing our spouse, which we can't. We may be a catalyst for change by growing ourselves and creating an environment of acceptance where change can occur, but we can't change our spouse.

The critical third step is learning to celebrate your differentness. This can be especially difficult if you've developed the habit of resenting some aspect of your spouse. The Bells suggest that when you recognize you're starting to think negative thoughts about your spouse, you should immediately stop. Remember that thoughts are much easier to control than feelings. Consistently negative thoughts inevitably produce negative feelings. Instead of dwelling on your partner's imperfections and what it is costing you, take the log out of your eye and think of what it costs your spouse to be married to you.

One of the great things about marriage is that you don't get to keep your imperfections to yourself. It's most helpful, and humbling, to then write down what those costs are. The second part of this step is to then express gratitude for your differentness. It's very possible that aspects of your spouse that annoy you are areas in which you are naturally weak. His carefree spirit balances your task focus. Her thoroughness balances your impulsiveness. Many of these differences are hard-wired into our souls. Sure we're fearfully and wonderfully made, but we're also imperfect and with plenty of room to grow.

Regardless of whether or not you employ the Bells' model for dealing with the rub, you have to come up with a way or ways of managing your perpetual issues. If you choose to focus on what's wrong with your spouse, that is what you will increasingly see, perhaps until it is all you will see. Only by putting the relationship ahead of your own agenda will you have the wisdom to identify the issues, the honesty to claim your own, the openness to discuss them, the perseverance to stay in the process, and the courage to grow. Did I mention that this is kind of unnatural?

Mark Allen is an Ironman legend. He won the event six times. But he didn't get to be number one until race number seven. He hung with it until his skill, conditioning, and race wisdom came together to elevate him from competitor to champion. So don't be surprised if your initial efforts at coping with perpetual problems aren't as effective as you'd hoped. Hang with it. It's a process of continuing to learn about yourself, your mate, and the two of you together in relationship. And never lose sight of the big picture.

## FORGIVENESS

There is a third component of conflict management. After love, it is probably the most often discussed tenet of the Christian faith. And after sex, it is probably the least understood tool in our relationship skill set.

"Forgiveness is love's toughest work," said the late Lewis Smedes, "and love's biggest risk." Regardless of how skilled you become at managing and resolving conflict, forgiveness is essential for your marriage to thrive. There will be times when you deeply disappoint and hurt each other. A careless oversight. A selfish act. A hurtful comment. It may not be intentional, and we may not understand why what we have done or not done is so painful, but we have hurt our spouse.

"Forgiveness is a decision to give up your perceived or actual right to get even with, or hold in debt, someone who has wronged you," say the authors of *Fighting for Your Marriage*. It is both an event and a process. We choose to give up our right to get even, and we continue to choose to give it up moment by moment, day by day.

"Forgiveness as a process means working through our own inner reactions until what was done to us no longer dominates us," says David Stoop. Forgiveness is built on the knowledge that you cannot change the past, but you will determine how it will affect the future. Forgiveness begins with ownership. The person who was wronged has to own the fact that he or she was hurt. Healthy ownership neither blows past the hurt to minimize everyone's discomfort—"Don't worry. It's not a big deal." Nor does it blow up the hurt to maximize everyone's discomfort—"How could you do this to me? I'll never get over this."

The person who wronged the other has to own the fact that what he or she did or didn't do inflicted hurt, whether intentional or not. Healthy ownership neither defends—"Come on, you're making a big deal out of nothing." Nor does it bury the act under a dumping of self-abuse—"You're right. It's all my fault."

Once ownership is established, it has to work its way past entitlement, defensiveness, self-deception, unhealthy guilt, self-pity, hardhearted self-righteousness, impatience, counterproductive and entrenched relational and personal habits, plain old ignorance, and the numerous distractions of busy lives and move toward a restored relationship that continues to move toward Christlikeness. Again, not the most natural way to behave.

Forgiveness, like most interactions, will conclude the way it started—in this case, ownership. The person who was wronged has to own the fact that for the relationship to move ahead, he or she has to give up the right to get even or to hold the other in debt. And the person who was in the wrong should admit, "I'm sorry. I was wrong. Please forgive me. This is where we go from here."

Where we go from here can be especially tough for men. Some research shows that men are more likely to continue to dwell on the hurt they suffered and ways they can hurt back, like treating their wives with a polite coldness or dragging in past or current areas of unrelated conflict. Like the transitions in triathlons, moving past conflict is an important skill. Smooth, efficient, purposeful, and on to the rest of your lives. Don't blow past conflict or dwell on the hurt. Both patterns are destructive in the long run.

Forgiveness: Love's toughest work. Love's greatest risk. Love's greatest reward.

If this all sounds hard and unnatural, it's because most of us learned conflict-management techniques on the fly. We learned how to get by and accomplish what was most important to us. If control was most important, we learned how to get through tense situations by powering up. If peace was most important, we learned to stick our heads in the sand until the issue "went away."

A 2.4-mile swim, followed by a 112-mile bike ride, followed by a 26.2-mile run—hard and unnatural for sure. But if you want *really hard* and *unusually unnatural,* try living with perpetual problems, resolving conflict in healthy ways, and forgiving each other. Whether it's a triathlon or conflict management in your marriage, they are no different from any other extreme endeavor. It's a question of belief. Do you believe the satisfaction you'll gain is worth the price you will pay? If you don't believe in the payoff, you won't make the investment.

"I have discovered this one incontrovertible truth about triathlon," says Eric Harr. "The more you challenge yourself, the deeper you dig, the more richly rewarded you are at the finish."

## SUMMARY

Conflict management is one of the most demanding components of an extreme marriage and one of the most necessary. Learning to identify and respectfully resolve conflict requires great skill. Finding the focus and strength to keep perpetual problems from undermining your relationship requires great perseverance. Finding the grace to forgive and the honesty to ask for forgiveness requires a clear picture of what you want your marriage to be. Like other extreme sports, the greater the challenge, the greater the reward for meeting it.

## FOR REFLECTION

1. How would you rate your skills at initiating a soft start-up in an attempt to resolve conflict?
2. Discuss a time when you went to someone to ask to be forgiven for something you did or didn't do.

# catch a wave, and you're sitting on top of the world

## sex is like big-wave surfing

> *There is no other sport that requires so little gear yet gives so much in terms of excitement, challenge, and soul satisfaction.*
>
> PETER DIXON, surfer and surfing instructor

most of us have seen it, either in person or on film: a huge wave rolls in from the ocean, spills over in a powerful curl, and thunders to a foamy end in the shallow water near the beach. A huge wave rolling in is at the same time both stunningly graceful and awesomely powerful. Ever wonder where the wave came from and how it got started?

If you're asking those questions from a little bulge of California coastline just south of San Francisco called Pillar Point, the answer to the first part is the North Pacific. The second part requires a little marine science.

It all starts with winter storms in the North Pacific. The storms' winds blow across the water. Rough patches are created on the surface as the winds' energy is transferred into the sea. As the blowing continues, the rough patches become small waves. The small waves combine with each other to become a swell. If the wind is strong and continues to blow, the swell will begin to move south toward California. That's when fetch, the distance a wave travels from its beginnings as a rough patch until its breakup on the shore, comes into play.

A fetch of about eight hundred miles is needed to produce waves that are big enough to surf. The swells coming out of the North Pacific head south essentially unencumbered, a fetch of about two thousand miles by the time they reach Pillar Point. As the swells move through the ocean, wavelength—the distance between the crests of two successive waves—helps determine the strength of the waves.

"The longer the wavelength, the more energy a wave can absorb from the wind and the higher the swell will grow," says Peter Dixon in *The Complete Guide to Surfing*. A large, well-organized swell can move through the ocean at twenty-five miles per hour as the waves organize into sets. The waves in front move faster, allowing the waves that follow to "draft," thereby conserving energy and maintaining their strength.

But it's not actually a wave of water that is moving down the coast. It's the energy that's moving through the water. Other than an up-and-down bob as the swell passes through, the water itself moves very little. Eventually the swell encounters an increasingly shallow coastal area in which the ocean's floor rises to a beach. And this is the beginning of the swell, which although it was barely discernible as it glided through the open water across the deep ocean floor, now becomes a visible wave.

As the floor rises, the energy and water simply run out of space. The lower part of the swell slows as it encounters a bottom that continues to rise. The rest of the swell continues forward as the water rises up to begin forming a wave. The wave begins to pitch forward. When the angle becomes so steep that the wave can no longer keep its form, the crest breaks and topples forward.

It's not just the rising ocean floor that determines the character of the wave. It's the way it rises up. In a coastal area with a gradually rising floor, the top of the wave will be slow in outpacing the bottom, resulting in rolling, easy-breaking waves. However, if the ocean's bottom rises abruptly, as in the case with an offshore reef, the bottom of the swell will slow abruptly, causing the wave to quickly rise, crest, and pitch forward. If conditions are right, these waves can reach heights of fifty feet and more.

And that's exactly what happens when the swells that originate in the North Pacific encounter the reef at Pillar Point, also known as Maverick's, the home of true big-wave surfing in the continental United States. When Maverick's is going off, the small and very skilled subculture known as big-wave surfers come from all over the country to get in on the action. Jon Krakauer estimated the number of true big-wave surfers to be less than a hundred worldwide.

The actual surfing part of a big-wave surfer's life is remarkably brief. Because of all the variables that must come together for the Maverick's to go off, Mark Warshaw, editor of *The Encyclopedia of Surfing,* estimates that a regular at Maverick's averages about twenty days of surfing a year. Though a ride can last forty to fifty seconds if conditions are right, the typical Maverick's ride lasts about fifteen seconds. A good day might include eight rides.

That means the average Maverick's surfer will probably spend less than an hour a year actually doing the thing he loves more than anything. The rest of the time he'll be thinking about it and preparing for it. It's a huge investment of time. It's risky. And if you're not a local, it can be expensive to get there. But oh what a payoff.

"It's created junkies out of most of us," admits Ken Bradshaw, the man who has ridden the highest wave ever surfed, an estimated eighty to eighty-five feet. "Surfing junkies, right? Our whole lives, we drop everything to go surfing, and we always will." In 1994 Bradshaw and his friend Mark Foo caught a flight from Hawaii to California because Maverick's was going off. It had backed off by the time they arrived on the morning of December 23, 1994. But just before noon, a series of ominous black lines appeared in the distance, announcing the arrival of a big-wave set.

Both surfers, already in the water, prepared to catch one of the monster waves. The first gently heaved them up as it passed under their boards. They both marked the second and paddled hard to catch it. As Bradshaw dug for the wave, he noticed Foo ahead and to his right. In a split second, Bradshaw backed off and let Foo have the wave. His takeoff was sound. He jumped up to his crouch, arms spread, well balanced. He was in control on one of the world's most challenging waves.

"The bottom configuration, the energy vectors—everything out there is incredibly complex," says Mark Renneker, a Maverick's veteran. "As a consequence, the wave goes through these strange kinks and lifts and drops, all happening in microseconds. You never know what's going to happen next."

What happened next was, the bottom fell out of Foo's wave, yanking his board to the left and throwing him off the front, down the face of the surging wall of water. A bad fall, for sure, but it happens all the time in big-wave surfing. Two more surfers caught the next wave, so none of the hundred or so people watching noticed that Foo failed to surface. He also failed to penetrate the surface far enough to escape getting hammered by the water and being pulled back up inside the wave itself.

Foo's body was discovered over an hour later, still leashed to a section of his broken board. Nobody knows for sure what happened. Was he knocked unconscious by his board? Did his leash catch on the coral, holding him under until he drowned?

"If you want to ride the ultimate wave, you have to be willing to pay the ultimate price," Foo often said.

Like most extreme sports, surfers keep ratcheting up the risk, continuing to test the threshold of what's possible. An early 1990s development literally jumped big-wave surfing to another level.

"Catching a wave" is more than just a phrase. Surfers don't just paddle out into the ocean and sit around on their boards until a wave comes along and picks them up. It's not like dragging a magnet through a pile of iron filings. A surfer does paddle out to wait for a wave set to come by. But once he sees one he wants to surf, he must paddle his board fast enough to overtake the wave. He must be able to catch it. And he has to catch it at the right place and at just the right time in the development of the crest. Since big waves move faster than smaller waves, the size of a wave that a surfer can catch is limited by how fast he can paddle.

A trio of surfers in Hawaii—Buzzy Kerbox, Darrick Doerner, and Laird Hamilton—began experimenting with using a boat to give surfers a running start at a wave. And "tow-in" surfing was born. In tow-in surfing, the surfer is pulled behind a personal watercraft, like a Jet Ski, much like a water-skier. As the surfer catches the wave, he drops the rope and finds himself near the top of a mountain of water, fifty feet high or more.

Wave power increases exponentially, so a fifty-foot wave is much more powerful than a thirty-footer. But it's not just height. Thickness is a more accurate indicator of a wave's lethal potential, and nowhere are the waves thicker than Tahiti's Teahupoo.

At Teahupoo, the ocean's floor rises abruptly from a depth of two thousand feet to just six feet in only a few hundred yards. Swells from Antarctica smash into the coral reef with such force that a wave doesn't actually peak. It shoots forcefully up, more like a powerful, surging wall than a classic curling wave. It is the world's thickest wave.

In August 2000, less than a month after a local big-wave surfer had been killed at Teahupoo, Hamilton dropped into a wave "so thick and powerful that it sucked the water in front of it down to 15 feet below sea level." "Dropped into" is an accurate description of what Hamilton encountered.

"The wave just [fell] away below him, until hundreds of feet of horizontal water…dropped into a 20-foot precipice," is how Daniel Duane describes it in *Men's Journal.* "A fast-forming canyon" of powerfully churning water. Hamilton quickly reached the bottom of the roaring wave. As he did, the entire top half lurched forward, a "single solid lip encasing him in a mineshaft with a 10-foot-thick wall in front and the ocean itself behind." He was unable to actually see the behemoth that was chasing him down. He knew only that he was in a huge wave and was extended to the very limit of his considerable abilities.

One wobble, one read that is not dead-on, one unexpected chop that he does not respond perfectly to, and Hamilton—a ripped six foot three, 220 pounds—will know what it's like to be "driven through a cheese grater by a steamroller." The handful of people watching could see the wave, and they knew that anything less than perfect would almost certainly result in Hamilton's death. Then water started swirling and surging through the tube, threatening to overtake him from behind as he continued to race across the face of the wave. It finally exploded forward, and Hamilton disappeared. Gone.

But only for a heart-stopping second or two. When the spray settled, he was still standing, the danger now over. So awed were his companions by what they had just witnessed that they were unable to speak.

"If you want to try this, you'd better be able to swim five miles, hold your breath for more than two minutes in churning water, and ride the biggest waves of your life in open ocean," warns Darrick Doerner, Hamilton's old tow-in friend, of the risk involved in surfing big waves.

When the significance of what he had just accomplished finally settled in Hamilton's heart and mind, he put his head between his knees and wept.

## CATCHING THE SEXUAL WAVE

Freedom and adventurousness are very likely what God had in mind for the sexual part of our marriage relationships. Sex is as powerful a force in our relationships as the big waves of Maverick's and Teahupoo. Sex is a place of enormous risk but also unparalleled satisfaction.

The sexual component of your marriage is arguably the most significant part of your entire relationship. That does not mean that having sex is the most important thing in your relationship. It is critically important but not for the reasons people normally think. Sex is so significant because it tells us where we really are instead of where we think we are. It is our relationship under the microscope. It reveals so much about us.

It tells us how we feel about God's creation. God created man and woman. He created both with a need for relationship. And though He created them to be different from one another (sometimes frustratingly different), His design was that they should be attracted to each other as complete physical, psychological, emotional, spiritual beings.

God also created sex, and it is nothing short of exceptional. His design was for us to experience an intense attraction to each other that culminated in our abandoning ourselves to one another in a sexual union. Naked and unashamed. Physically and emotionally. Who we are and who we are not. Generously giving to and receiving of each other. Fully delighting in each other not as strictly sexual partners but as complete people. Two becoming one. Sex was God's idea, and He wants us to enjoy it.

But He knew the awesome power of what He created. He also knew that the only way to protect the people involved, the integrity of the gift, and the intensity of the experience was to place it in the context of a mutually committed, mutually serving, mutually respectful, mutually grace-extending, mutually understanding, mutually loving marriage relationship. It's what we have been calling an extreme marriage.

People debate whether God's primary purpose for sexual intimacy was procreation or recreation—having children or enjoying each other. In *Sacred Sex,* Tim Gardner argues that though both can result, the ultimate purpose is even bigger.

"The essence of sexual intimacy can never be enjoyed, nor can true and lasting sexual fulfillment occur, until a wife and a husband grasp the truth that the number-one purpose of sex is neither pro-creation nor recreation, but unification.… This unification is the celebration of the soul-deep bond that is present when a couple knows and experiences the certainty that they are together perma-nently [see chapter 5] for a divine purpose [see chapter 2]."

Gardner suggests that we celebrate communion to remind us of God's covenant with us. We should celebrate our sexual relationship with our spouse the same way, as a reminder of our covenant with each other. Is it possible that a rich and satisfying sexual relationship with your spouse can help you become more like Jesus?

These images are a mental train wreck for many people, because our attitudes about sex reveal how influenced we are by the world in which we live. Can we view sex as God's good and perfect creation, or are we more influenced by what we hear on the radio, read in the magazines, see on television, and quite possibly have experienced ourselves? The further our experiences have taken us from the origi-nal design, the harder we will have to work to reclaim what God intended and the harder we will have to fight to protect it.

All of us have been bombarded with sexual messages that are so distorted that God's gift of sexuality is unrecognizable. And many of us have made choices that took us even further from the ideal. Some of us have used sex for our own physical pleasure, regardless of the emotional and spiritual consequences for ourselves and our part-ners. Some of us have used it for our ego gratification. Some of us have used it to acquire something we really wanted—attention, approval, possessions.

When we were children, before we even had a sexual awareness, seeds were planted that may have borne a bitter fruit in adulthood. From attitudes about the harmlessness of fantasy and pornography to the notion that sex is primarily a physical act without emotional consequences, the culture has shaped our individual sexuality. From what constitutes physical beauty to what techniques we should employ to attract and arouse a partner to ensure that you both achieve an orgasm, the world has been our instructor.

Our culture continues to "teach" us every day. The world has done a masterful job of simultaneously trivializing sex and raising it to the level of cultural idolatry. We've reduced sexual intimacy to the level of being a common expectation of even casual relationships while at the same time suggesting it is an urge so strong that regular sexual release is a biological need.

It's anything but God's view of sex as a holy, life-giving expression of profound love for a complete person.

## THE BURDEN OF POPULAR STEREOTYPES

We live in a culture driven by media images. Physical characteristics, worldly attitudes, and monetary success become the standards by which we determine a man's or woman's attractiveness. And the bar is set pretty high for women, with a disproportionate emphasis on physical characteristics, and men, with a disproportionate emphasis on worldly attitudes and success.

In our sex-saturated world, the images that excite men often discourage women. Men need to know that many women, regardless of their age or apparent physical attractiveness, are uncomfortable with their bodies. The women's magazines have as many pictures of young, thin, surgically and cosmetically enhanced, professionally photographed models as the men's magazines.

Women are as conscious of the standard as men are. And they are often more aware of the gap between what they look like and what they are told the ideal woman looks like. It started when they were young girls and continued as they grew into women. Dissatisfaction is huge business.

And women need to know that the classic image of the decisive, successful-in-all-I-do, look-at-the-lifestyle-I-provide man creates a fantasy ideal that many men feel compelled to pursue at the cost of a connected relationship. Our sense of worth may be tied up with achievement and acquisition. Success in business and lifestyle may be easier to measure and more widely respected than success in marriage. Performance is what matters. But whatever we provide may not seem like enough. Maybe it's natural competitiveness. Maybe it's insecurity. Maybe it's self-centered desires. Whatever the reasons, men's dissatisfaction is huge business too.

In either case, a spouse can ease a mate's discomfort and insecurities by focusing on him or her as a complete person who has many attractive qualities. As you observe those qualities, tell your wife or husband. Let your partner know that you notice him or her and are attracted to the person, not the sex or lifestyle he or she provides. Offer reassurance and encouragement. Express your attraction for the complete emotional, psychological, spiritual, and sexual person. Express it in ways that are sexual and nonsexual. The important thing is to express it. Help each other out with the burden of one another's discomfort.

Focus on your spouse as the sole source of your own sexual and emotional stimulation. If you're a man, your wife becomes your standard, not the continually changing stream of never-aging, physically perfect models and actresses whose job it is to look great. If you're a woman, your husband becomes your standard. The relationship each of you should dwell on is the one you want to have with your spouse, not relationships with fantasy men or women or with real people at work or the kids' soccer games. Obviously through work, organizations that we're part of, and groups of friends, we will be in relationships with people we find sexually, emotionally, and mentally stimulating. We have to be constantly vigilant to keep those relationships within appropriate boundaries.

It is good that both women and men are motivated by a desire to be physically attractive for their spouse. It is also good that women and men approach life with the same kind of decisiveness, purposefulness, and intensity that Jesus displayed. They are part of a healthy, complete attraction. Our standard is our spouse, and we should focus on being attracted to them and being attractive for them. But we should never use loving acceptance by our spouse as an excuse for indifference to our appearance or mediocrity in our approach to life. Neither should we be driven by a need to live up to external standards imposed on us by the world we live in.

## COMMUNICATING ABOUT SEX

Our approach to sexual intimacy tells us where we are in our ability to communicate openly and honestly with each other. If our marriages are built on a foundation of trust, seeking to understand, and serving in love, we can learn about making love from the person who is probably best qualified to teach on the subject—our spouse. But we have to be willing to ask. We have to be willing to listen. And we have to be willing to change, if that's required.

That conversation will not happen if both the husband and the wife haven't participated in building that foundation and are not motivated by a genuine desire to understand and serve. We have to be willing to respectfully and lovingly engage in a potentially uncomfortable conversation about a mutually vulnerable subject that our culture has trained us to avoid altogether or to speak of in either strangely clinical terms or disrespectful slang.

Since the conversation may be initially uncomfortable, why not use instructional aids? No, not the thinly disguised pornographic how-to videos in the magazine ads. Educate your partner and yourself by reading together and discussing books like *Sacred Sex* and Cliff and Joyce Penner's *Getting Your Sex Life Off to a Great Start*. Learn about the attitude of oneness as well as the techniques of sex. Discover the complete sexual experience that God wants you to delight in.

In *Sacred Sex,* Amy Gardner advises husbands that for a wife to enter into sex as a holy encounter, she needs to know her husband deeply. Being known by him is essential as well. She also warns husbands that attempts to initiate sex may feel like a demand if a foundation of connection is not in place.

Tim Gardner counsels wives that a husband's desire for sex is not always just about sex. It's often a desire to feel loved, though many men wouldn't necessarily phrase it that way. This fact that men have a need to feel loved helps explain why a man can feel so hurt if his wife isn't receptive to the idea of making love. It feels more like rejection of the person than postponement of the event.

A husband needs to know that his wife probably sees her world as a much more integrated whole than he does. Seemingly unrelated aspects of her life—relationships at work, issues with her children, challenges that friends or family are facing—can have an effect on how she feels about her sexual relationship. And a wife should know that her husband's sexual desire may be completely unaffected by the same things that preoccupy her.

A lot goes into a couple's sexual relationship. But a lot goes into the formation of a big wave. And a lot goes into developing the skills to be a big-wave surfer. It's a complex, risky business for a brief payoff. But surfers understand that the real payoff is the satisfaction they gain, so they invest in what they enjoy. It's important for husbands and wives to understand that in order to receive the relationship satisfaction they need, they must invest in communicating and understanding each other.

Sexual desire is built into both the man and the woman. If we don't feel attracted to our mate, we have to ask ourselves why. Are our schedules too jammed? Are we taking the concept of sacred sex lightly and not purposefully celebrating our covenant with each other? Has the world we live in placed some kind of standard or expectation in us that we're holding our mate up to? Is there a missing component of emotional connection and respect?

Many of these ideas fall into common sexual stereotypes. A reason that sexual stereotypes exist is that they are often true. Often, but not always. And maybe never true in your relationship. What is important is that you gain an understanding of each other and figure out what is true in your relationship.

## ENTITLEMENT

Sex reveals how we're doing in our battle with entitlement. A man may feel that as a husband he is entitled to sexual intimacy. In fact, it may be the area in which a man feels most entitled. A woman may feel she's entitled to emotional connection. And both would be right. Both expectations are reasonable and healthy, necessary under normal circumstances for the marriage to flourish. In God's design for the marriage relationship, men and women both need sexual intimacy and emotional connection, though probably not in equal proportions. The two are inextricably linked.

But what happens when a reasonable expectation is not met? When a wife doesn't meet her husband's sexual expectations, does he feel entitled to insist on sex or use it as a justification to escape to a world of fantasy, pornography, and masturbation? And when a husband doesn't meet a wife's emotional expectations, does she feel entitled in withholding herself from their sexual relationship or pursuing emotional connection with someone else? Does either feel entitled to somehow withdraw from the relationship, withholding the expressions of love, support, and encouragement that contribute to the emotional connection both need to thrive?

A question each married couple has to answer is whether challenges in life and their relationship will inflame their sense of entitlement or increase their commitment to understand their spouse and serve him or her in love.

Demanding and withholding are flip sides of the coin of entitlement. In our day-to-day lives, these themes play out much more subtly, but they are frequent temptations for all married couples. And they will often show up in your sexual relationship.

Sex also tells where we are in our marriage in general, because demanding and withholding don't consistently enter the picture of a healthy marriage. You may feel entitled to demand or withhold, but to do so violates the standard of Christlikeness. And though you will have isolated incidents of selfishness, they should be exactly that, isolated incidents.

Are you playing games of demanding and withholding, or are you lovingly giving of yourself and gratefully receiving of your spouse? The clear and consistent trend in your marriage should be toward focusing on what you can give to the relationship, both physically and emotionally, rather than what you can get from it.

It is unrealistic of you to expect your spouse to give freely and generously in sexual or emotional ways if you have not given with that same kind of freedom and generosity. Unfortunately, it is easier to keep score on physical intimacy than on an emotional connection.

Sexual attraction is a natural part of a strong marriage between an emotionally healthy husband and wife. We're supposed to be attracted to each other. It's part of God's design. If we're not, we have to ask ourselves why.

Is there some need you haven't identified that is unmet? How about a need you have identified that your spouse has not yet met? Is there an area of resolvable conflict that hasn't been resolved? Is there an unresolvable "perpetual" issue that you've not yet come to terms with, and so you continue to squander time and energy trying to change your spouse or resenting him or her? Are there issues in your past you haven't dealt with that keep you from fully enjoying the present? Are you so consumed by various necessary or worthwhile endeavors—children, work, recreational pursuits, involvement with church and other groups—that you have neither the time or energy to invest in a mutually satisfying sexual relationship?

"If you want to ride the ultimate wave, you have to be willing to pay the ultimate price," Mark Foo often said. The ultimate wave in marriage is not sex but true connection. Our sexual relationship as a husband and wife is critically important, but like the Maverick's surfers who orient their lives around big waves, the time we spend making love is small. But so much goes into it.

If our desire is not for just a pleasurable sexual experience but for a satisfying sexual relationship, we have to be willing to pay the ultimate price. We have to be willing to give of ourselves.

"Being sexually intimate while being fully present in mind, body and soul is costly," says Tim Gardner. But oh what a payoff. Naked and unashamed. Physically and emotionally. Who we are and who we are not. Extreme companionship.

## Summary

It's very possible that God's intent for our sexual relationship was that it bring us together as a reminder of our covenant with each other. It's supposed to unite us, the physical and emotional pleasure being a reflection of the relationship itself. But clarifying our view of sex and preserving it is a daily discipline. And so is doing the things necessary to make it a vibrant part of your marriage.

## For Reflection

1. Is there anything stopping you from buying a book like *Sacred Sex* or *Getting Your Sex Life Off to a Great Start* so you and your spouse can discover the fullness of the sexual relationship God desires for you?

2. What could you do to be a better sexual partner for your spouse? But remember, sex isn't just about sex.

# Rapids, as in Fast Moving

## Change is like whitewater kayaking

*What separates the brilliant experts from the rest of us
mortals is that the experts simply execute those strokes
in all situations, no matter how intense or perilous.*

GORDON GRANT, whitewater kayaker

Shangri-la. Utopia. A place of great beauty and peaceful-
ness. Paradise on earth.

And how does one get there? The journey begins with a flight
to Tibet, home of the Tsangpo Gorge. The gorge is a place of myth
and mystery, the inspiration for the Shangri-la of James Hilton's
novel *Lost Horizon*.

But where the real journey begins is a small Tibetan town called
Pe on a bank of the Yarlung Tsangpo River, near the beginning of
the gorge. From there all that separates you from Shangri-la and the
happiness and inner harmony it offers is about 45 miles of the
world's most dangerous white water. The river drains the northern
slope of the Himalayas and cuts between the 25,446-foot Namcha

Barwa and the 23,462-foot Gyala Pelri. It enters the gorge at about 9,000 feet and emerges 150 miles later at 1,000 feet, dropping 100 to 200 feet per mile in some sections.

In February 2002 a group of seven of the world's most elite big-water kayakers stood on the bank of the river, ready to begin an attempted first descent of what has been called the Everest of rivers. It's not that others hadn't tried. Many had. But none had succeeded. The most recent serious attempt, four years prior, ended just beyond the halfway point when one of the team members drowned in a particularly treacherous section of white water.

"You have to be 'spot on' to run Class V water. The price for not being exactly where you want to be can be high," advises Stephen U'Ren. Ranging in age from twenty-four to thirty, these men were young enough to be jazzed by the challenge and old enough to have an idea of what lay ahead. All had spent much of their lives in kayaks and still paddled more than two hundred days a year. After sealing themselves into their boat cockpits with their spray skirts, they glided away from the certainty of land and into the forty-degree water. Near the end of the first day, they encountered their toughest challenge so far.

The first three kayakers paddled hard into the first set of hydraulics, clearing them without incident. Willie Kern charged into the next set. The swirling current pushed him off his line and flipped him. He rolled back up, just in time to disappear into a massive hole. But he was quickly back to the surface, shaking his head to regain his senses. Once recovered, he dug hard for the safe water on the left. Dustin Knapp was next around the corner, and he was swallowed by the same hole. Flipped him, too, but forty feet to the right. He rolled up and joined Kern. The river was unlike anything any of them had ever experienced.

It was one of the eleven sets of rapids they encountered that day. A solid day's work that left them exhausted by nightfall. They rested and contemplated what they had gotten themselves into. The next day they would be on the river again in an expedition that took thirty-three days to complete.

The team came to an especially steep and threatening drop on day four. Six of the world's finest whitewater kayakers picked up their boats and portaged. Confidence can get you through the rapids; hubris can get you killed. The seventh climbed a boulder to scout the section. After concluding it was runnable, he returned to his boat and seal-launched into the river, without advising his teammates.

Swept along by the current, he threaded his way through a boulder maze. He saw the line he wanted for his flight over a ten-foot waterfall and hit it with precision, dropping into the frigid water below for a few mind-numbing moments. He popped to the surface and paddled hard left into an eddy that was surging against an unyielding rock wall—a bad place to be in a thrashing river like the Tsangpo. There was no time to rest or think. The longer he stayed, the more certain the relentless river would find some imbalance to exploit. He flipped, rolled back up, and saw the line he thought would give him the best chance of escape. No margin for error. He sprinted hard into the main current, narrowly avoiding a crashing wave and driving through another. He was clear, as safe as a person can be in a whitewater section of the world's most powerful river. The whole near-fatal episode took less than sixty pulse-racing seconds, and afterward the team agreed that there would be no more impulsive runs.

Whitewater kayaks are shorter and wider than sea kayaks. They are designed for maneuverability. They turn easily and are not self-correcting. They go where the current takes them or to where they are guided. Beginning kayakers are often frustrated by how difficult it is to paddle one on a straight line. They become more frustrated when they enter even minor rapids and miss moves, end up in places they didn't want to be, or tip over. Their inability to maneuver kayaks with the timing, skill, and precision they've observed in more experienced kayakers can be discouraging.

Unlike many extreme sports, you don't depend on yourself for movement in whitewater kayaking. The current will move you. It most certainly will. In big water like the Tsangpo, it will twist you and turn you. It will shoot you up and pull you under. It will roar in your ears and smack you in the face. It will grab you, flip you, 180 you, and pop you back to the surface, facing upstream. It will drive you into unyielding river boulders and drag you into churning, chaotic holes.

No, movement is never a problem in white water. Once a kayaker is in Class V rapids, he can't stop if he is tired, in pain, or off-line. The river doesn't stop and wait for the kayaker to rest, correct, or recover. It just keeps going. Though a kayaker may find an eddy in which he is safe, eventually he will have to deal with the river. If you don't control your kayak, the current will, without much regard for you.

Because rivers are always moving and kayaks are designed for maneuverability, river kayaking is an exercise in minicorrection. And whitewater kayaking demands nearly continual adjustment. The kayaker is responding to what is going on right now, making an adjustment for some unexpected wave surge or compensating for the move he didn't hit perfectly, all the while setting himself up for what is coming.

In whitewater kayaking, you tend to move toward what you are looking at. If there is a huge rock in the middle of the river creating a treacherous current pattern, you stare at it. It's like a car wreck ahead of you that ties up traffic. You swear you won't look at it when you pass, but as you approach, you slow down. You look. You can't help yourself.

If it's just one rock and not too big, you might be able to slip past, even with poor technique. Funny thing about rocks in rivers, they tend to congregate. They form boulder gardens. And as water rushes through a rock-strewn boulder-garden section of the channel, you get white water.

The best kayakers know to focus on where they want to go, not on the boulder and the churning, frothing water. When scouting the section, they determine the safe line through the rapids. Then they follow that line of sight to some fixed point. That fixed point is what they focus on. That is what they are paddling to.

Inexperienced kayakers stare at the big rock and the currents, even though they know they should be focusing on the safe line through the rapids and doing the little things necessary to make it through. It's hypnotic. And as you stare, you get pulled toward it. And as you get pulled toward it, you start to get off balance. And as you get off balance, you struggle to right yourself in increasingly fast-moving, swirling white water. You overcompensate, and now you're in real trouble. Unless you're experienced, disciplined, and skilled, you forget all about that safe line you were trying to thread. You flip into survival mode instead of concentrating on performing the techniques necessary to solve the problem. And as you flip into survival mode…well, good luck.

"Few other sports require the processing of so much data so fast. Survival depends on split-second decisions, both reflexive and deliberate—and not just one or two in a drop, but continuously, in a dynamic flow of constant recalibration." A single small mistake in a whole day's paddling on a powerful whitewater river can be fatal.

If there is ever a time to be in the zone, dialed in, and on top of your game, whitewater kayaking is it. Those are the times when the game seems to slow down. The athletes do all the right things at just the right time. Complex activities are performed as an integrated whole, not a mechanistic assembling of related tasks. If they make a mistake, they recover quickly and unselfconsciously and return to that level of optimum performance.

Like all extreme sports, challenge is part of the deal in whitewater kayaking. A kayaker learns what he can about a river by talking to others and scouting the tough sections himself. Because the Tsangpo had never been successfully run and much of it had never been seen by Westerners, the expedition had to rely on satellite images. A kayaker has an idea of what he'll encounter and where, but there are far too many variables for him to know exactly what will be going on when he is in the water or how he will respond. The ever-changing conditions on the river make it interesting. It's the certainty of uncertainty that makes it fun.

## Marriage White Water

Your married life will be much like the river. There will be long, calm sections of peaceful paddling that might bore the risktaker in your relationship but delight the one who prefers smooth and steady. There will also be whitewater sections when changes in your lives swirl and rush. "Smooth and steady" may be anxious, while "risktaker" is delighted and pumped for the action.

Know that you will experience challenges in your married life. Absolutely, without a doubt, count on it. Challenges will most often come in the form of changes. Your relationship skill set—love languages, identifying and resolving conflict that can be resolved, living with one another in increasingly understanding and loving ways— will determine how well you respond to challenges. If your habits of serving one another in love (Galatians 5:13) are strong, the swirl of change won't rattle you. If there is ever a time to be in the zone, dialed in, on top of your marriage game, a time of change is it.

From where you are now, the end of your life may seem pretty far off. And it probably is. The Bureau of the Census tells us that you're probably going to live about seventy-four years if you're a man, about eighty if you're a woman. You can do the math. That means if you're married, you'll be spending the next thirty, forty, fifty years with the same person. The person you are married to today is not even the same person he or she will be in ten years. Neither are you.

Look around you. How's your health? How about your mate's? And how about your folks' health? Your spouse's parents' health? Do you come from good, hearty stock, or does the gene pool raise some concerns? Are both sets of parents still alive and in good health? Are you ready to become a caregiver to them? Any skeletons in the family closet—maybe abuse or alcoholism—that might have a profound but not yet recognized effect on your sweetie?

Either of you already have any children? Are you planning on having any, and if so, how many? What happens if child number two becomes numbers two and three? Aren't they cute? What happens if you have a special-needs child? Are you going to be okay if, for whatever reason, you can't have children of your own?

Whoa, look at those intersecting lines on your budget graph—one a noticeable decline in income if one of you decides to be a stay-at-home parent and the other line in steep ascent as expenses spike with the arrival of your stay-at-home infant. Do you think the emotional, psychological, and relational world of a stay-at-home parent might be dramatically different from what he or she knew as a working person?

Children are a vortex of change. From pregnancy to the arrival of a completely dependent infant to the independence of walking to the rapid progression of preschool, kindergarten, and grade school. Changes in a child mean changes for parents. And oh, did you notice how different child number two is from child number one? Next they're going over to friends' houses and then on to high school. One day they come home brandishing their, *gulp,* driver's permit. Soon there's the final, potentially testing summer before they head off for the big change, the see-you-on-parents'-weekend change of college.

That great sucking sound may not be just savings getting siphoned off but also the relational buffer you and your spouse had. Wait a minute, who is that person? And who are you? What happened to that project called "kids" that you've both been so consumed with? How are you going to handle the confusion of midlife readjustments for you and your spouse?

Do you think you will be living in your current home, city, and state twenty years from now? How rewarding, both financially and emotionally, is your current business? If you're an employee, how stable is your employer? How are you going to handle the loss of income if your job is one they're planning to downsize?

On the other hand, congratulations are in order for your promotion at work, the one you've worked so hard for. The one you find challenging and financially rewarding and, uh-oh, the one that brings you into daily contact with that co-worker you've always thought was attractive. Is travel, along with its distractions and temptations, part of your move up? Does your absence create just enough of an opening that your children begin to lose themselves in their own challenges?

What happens when the nicks and dings and general deterioration of forty, fifty, sixty, seventy, or even eighty years show up on your body and mind and your spouse?

Those are some, but by no means all, of the situations you may encounter along the way. All of them involve change. Circumstances will change. You will change. Changes often intensify or diminish existing needs and expectations. Or changes may lead you to discover different needs and expectations.

## The White Water of Change

Rivers exist because water flows from a higher point to a lower point. Three things determine the speed at which it flows. First, volume—the amount of water in a river channel. Second, gradient—the difference between those higher and lower points. Third, river structure—the width and depth of the channel and any obstructions that are in it. The combination of all three in the Tsangpo makes it a wild, powerful, and thrashing river. Any one of those can cause a current to accelerate. That's why they're called rapids. And a combination of all three? Let the games begin.

Change is the white water in your marriage. It is defined by author and change expert William Bridges as a shift in your external circumstances—the birth of a child, a new job, the medical condition you suddenly discover, the unexpected death of a parent. Change is the rock in your river disrupting what was normal. Some you can control; some you can't. Some are mere stones, so small that life glides right over them. Others are boulders, big enough to create holes so powerful they're called "keepers" because they can grab a kayaker and hold him under, often till he drowns.

All changes carry the potential for stress. Generally, the greater the change, the greater the potential for stress. In times of stress, you go with what you know best. So what do you know best? Have you worked to develop the habit of thinking about how the changes affect your spouse and how you can serve him or her? Or is your reflex to think first of yourself and be more concerned with how the changes affect you? If you have not developed good habits and strong technique in the calm stretches of the river, you won't have what it takes in the whitewater sections of change.

As predictably as rocks congregate in a riverbed, changes often come in groups. Each change requires some adjustment. Each adjustment means the potential for error, being a little off balance or not correctly positioned for the next change. And as the changes increase, in either number or significance, so does the skill required to successfully run the rapids.

Most likely, one change won't flip you, but it might get you off balance. You start to focus on how the changes are affecting you and how you're feeling and less on how your partner is feeling. You might make the second change also but get a little further off balance. Now it's becoming easier to focus on yourself and harder to focus on your spouse. Your technique is breaking down and your eyes are darting. Maybe it's the third change that really gets your attention and engages your sense of entitlement. You deserve better.

If you have not done business with your sense of entitlement, you could find yourself dwelling on what you deserve. If you have not identified how your self-centeredness shows up in your marriage, you might focus on your spouse's shortcomings. If you haven't formed strong habits of servanthood in your dating relationship and early marriage, then you may find yourself on that familiar path of least resistance leading to control or approval seeking.

## The Safe Line

So what is it you're trying to achieve in marriage? Did you answer that one yet? Happiness? Approval? Pleasure? Image management? Self-preservation? Worldly success? Christlikeness?

Becoming more like Jesus is the fixed point on the riverbank. That's what you're focusing on. That's what you're paddling toward. Unless becoming more like Jesus is what you're trying to achieve, you'll probably get caught up in the distracting swirl of life. It will be easy to fall back into the old patterns of having things your way.

Change is the external shift in circumstances, the new reality. It is an event. It is followed by what Bridges calls the neutral zone. It's a period of confusion and stress. Depending on the significance of the change, nothing may be the same. The old roles, the old ways of doing things, the old ways of seeing yourself—they can all be gone.

You have not yet identified or become comfortable with new roles, new ways of doing things, new ways of looking at yourself. A transition has not been made.

Transition is the internal adjustment we make to that new reality. Okay, you have a child. What is the new reality in your family? What do you need to do differently? What does your mate need from you today in order to make his or her transition? What does he or she need in order to continue the process of becoming more like Jesus? And what does your newborn need from you?

"Every transition begins with an ending," says Bridges. "We have to let go of the old thing before we can pick up the new." Many people are uncomfortable letting go of what has been. For many people, the certainty of what has been, regardless of how unsatisfactory it is, is more comfortable than the uncertainty of what might be.

Whitewater kayaking is a continual exercise in minicorrection. So is adapting to life changes. How do you need to think differently in order to adjust to the new reality but still pursue your overarching goal of becoming more like Jesus? What do you need to do differently today so that your family continues to move ahead? What little things are necessary to keep your loving and serving on track?

Remember, you're not just adapting to this change, you're setting yourself up for what's ahead on the river. Where you end up, whether it's next year or in ten years, will be determined by the choices you make today and how well you execute them.

No two rivers are the same, and no river is the same on different days. In life, each change and resulting transition are unique. Just because the same people are involved doesn't mean there is a can't-miss formula you can apply to all changes. Whatever is going on in your lives has affected you, even if only slightly. You're different, maybe a lot different. So is your spouse. Changes cause other changes.

Changes are events that happen, boulders in the river that disrupt what was normal. But once the transitions are made, what was change is the new normal. Each change requires a transition, and afterward you may notice the river is running faster. Life takes on a momentum of its own. Each variable—husband, wife, children, extended family—adds volume to the river, which can increase the difficulty of the next whitewater section of change.

Contrary to what people often say, a husband and wife don't just drift apart. You need to understand that the currents of life are not favorable to easy relationship. The currents of life swirl. They can distract you and divide you, possibly drown you. Unless you are purposeful about continuing to build your marriage in spite of changes, unless you transition with your marriage in mind, you will flounder. There is no point in your marriage at which you can kick back and say, "Done." Your circumstances are always changing, even if not noticeably. There's a lot of truth in the old saying, "The only thing that's constant is change."

The white water of change is a certainty in your marriage. It's not a question of if; it's a question of when and how many and how big and, most important, how you will respond. Will you panic in the rapids and focus on yourself instead of Jesus, the fixed point? Will you serve yourself or your mate?

Marriage can be your Shangri-la but only if you successfully run the white water of change.

## Summary

You can and should plan for change, even though you don't know how you'll respond until you're in the change. Develop your relationship skills to the point of habits, because once the changes start happening and your lives run faster, you'll go with the relationship patterns you know best. Will they be old, potentially ineffective, and self-serving behaviors, or will they be new patterns of serving one another in love?

## For Reflection

1.  What two relationship skills do you feel most confident you'll use even in the white water of life change?
2.  What one skill do you most need to develop?

# Reaching the void

Persevering in marriage is like an epic survival adventure

> *We had sat in the same spot six days earlier....*
> *All our keen excitement, and the healthy strong feel*
> *in our bodies, had become an empty memory.*
> SIMON YATES, high-altitude mountaineer

e climbed because it was fun…just brilliant fun," explained Joe Simpson. "But every now and then it went wildly wrong. And then it wasn't."

Simpson and Simon Yates, his climbing partner, had come to the Peruvian Andes in an attempt to be the first to summit 21,000-foot Siula Grande via the 4,500-foot West Face. Their plan was to spend ten days on various climbs in the vicinity while they acclimatized and learned the weather patterns.

This was not like climbing in the popular and congested Alps. Except for Richard, an international nomad who accepted their invitation to see the Andes up close by serving as the watchman for their base camp, Simpson and Yates were alone. They were not climbing for the cameras or corporate sponsors. The risks and rewards would be theirs, and theirs alone. And the risks would be considerable since they were climbing fast and light, in the pure Alpine ethic. They would carry only enough supplies for the time they planned to spend on the mountain. They would sleep in snow caves they dug into the side of the mountain at the end of their climbing day rather than in a tent they carried with them. Their margin for error was thin. "Four days you reckon, then?" Richard asked, as the climbers prepared to leave base camp.

"Five at the outside," said Simon, "and if we're not back after a week, you'll be the proud owner of all our gear." They all recognized it as the sort of bravado that often precedes endeavors of great risk. They climbed through the first day without incident, dug a snow hole just beneath the face, and bedded down for the night. The second day's climb began at 5:00 a.m. and ended in the dark at 10:30, four and a half hours after the sun had set. They were spent from a day of swinging their ice axes, front pointing on their crampons, crossing a long and dangerously steep ice field, and enduring numerous falling rocks and chunks of ice.

On the third day, the two survived a fall by Simon, a battle with thick, 5-foot-long icicles, spindrift avalanches, and a section where Joe, unnerved by the exposure of standing on an open face with a 4,000-foot drop at his back, stood temporarily paralyzed with fear. Their day ended at 11:00 p.m. in a precarious snow hole they dug only 300 vertical feet from the summit. The outside temperature was minus twenty, colder with the wind, as they finished the last of their freeze-dried meals.

The fourth day was clear with no wind, an ideal day to summit, which they did with relative ease. After celebrating with a few summit photos and some chocolate, they began to plan their descent.

"It looks hairy," said Simpson as the pair viewed the route that included steep razor edges, frighteningly corniced sections, and treacherous flutings. Compounding the danger were the storm clouds that were already beginning to cover sections of their route down. Within forty-five minutes they found themselves in a whiteout. They continued. They each had a fall that certainly would have been fatal had they not been roped together. The danger and constant tension was exhausting. Tired and cold, they dug another snow cave and slipped into their sleeping bags for the night.

By the fifth day they were growing increasingly eager to get off the mountain. The novelty of the adventure had long since worn off, and the satisfaction of their accomplishment could only be fully enjoyed once safely down from the face. Joe began the day by leading through deep, powdery snow. He soon encountered a vertical ice cliff, about 25 feet high. He found a section not quite vertical and only 20 feet above the base. This was the point at which he chose to make his descent. He got his ice axes to bite into the ice, slipped his legs over the edge, and kicked his crampons into the wall. As he began his climb down, he heard the ice crack.

Before he even realized what was happening, his feet struck the ice at the base of the cliff. Unprepared for the sudden impact, his legs were locked, and the abrupt stop drove his lower right leg through his knee, shattering his kneecap. He catapulted down the slope, headfirst on his back.

Since they were roped together, Simon felt the first jerk of the rope and immediately planted his ice axes into the snow to brace himself. Joe was yanked to a sudden stop. When he recovered his senses, he looked down and saw his right knee violently twisted into a grotesquely distorted zigzag. Pain and nausea swamped him as the severity of the injury and what it meant were immediately apparent to him.

When Simon first saw his fallen partner and learned his leg was broken, his immediate, matter-of-fact, unspoken response was, "You're dead...no two ways about it." Joe had already come to a similar conclusion. And even though Joe's death was a mutually rec-ognized, foregone conclusion, both men knew they had to try to get down.

Climbing down was an impossibility, at least for Joe. Both men were aware that Simon could safely descend, but he stayed. They chose not to dwell on the accident but on a course of action. They figured out a belaying system. One of them would dig a bucket seat into the snow for Simon to anchor himself and lower Joe down the side of the mountain using two 150-foot ropes they'd knotted together.

It was a desperately dangerous system, given the tenuous nature of Simon's improvised belay anchor on the open face of the mountain. It was also desperately painful for Joe, given his inability to control his injured leg. His boot would catch the slope, producing "sickening, gristly crunches" as the shattered bones grated against each other. Each snag sent hot stabs of searing pain shooting up his leg. He sobbed. He cursed. He screamed. He endured. It was either that or die.

They continued their pattern. Simon lowered. Joe endured the agony, after which he would dig the next seat for Simon, who was climbing down. And they'd begin again. Against all odds, it was working. Even as an afternoon storm arrived. Even as their fingers began to grow numb with frostbite. Even as increasingly large spin-drift avalanches momentarily engulfed them. Even as the sun set, the temperature dropped, and the winds picked up. Seven lowerings and two rappels had moved them down nearly 2,700 feet of the esti-mated 3,000 they figured they'd need to get to the relatively flat safety of the glacier. They were almost there.

Their confidence was growing and their hope rising as they began their eighth lowering. As Joe once again disappeared down the slope into the snowy night, he noticed that he was sliding faster. The slope was suddenly steeper, and his speed continued to pick up. He made a futile attempt to brake with his arms as his mind raced through the possibilities for this sudden acceleration in their rhythm. He knew he was rapidly approaching a drop-off. He *had* to stop. He shouted a warning to Simon, knowing his friend probably wouldn't hear. He attempted to brake with his ice ax, but the snow was too loose. He dug his left crampon into the snow with the same result. Suddenly he was no longer sliding on the snow but falling backward through the air.

He jerked to a stop, his body spinning on the taut rope and arced into an awkward crescent, facing up into another cascade of spindrift. Though still spinning, he pulled himself up to a seated position and began to assess the situation. The edge he had gone over was steeply overhanging and 15 feet above him. As he looked below, through the darkness and flurries, he thought he saw the dark outline of a crevasse. But it was at least 100 feet away. The ice wall directly in front of him was 6 feet away.

In the best circumstances, it would have been extremely difficult for Simon to pull him up. There was no chance of rescue from above. The ice wall was out of reach. And even if he had reached it, climbing it would have been impossible with only one good leg. There was no chance of self-rescue.

And there was no chance of communication. They were separated by the distance, the wind, the snow, the night, and now the edge of the ice cliff. Though Simon could tell by the sudden jerk and constant pressure on the rope that Joe had gone over an edge, he had no way of knowing whether it was the edge of a 10-foot or a 100-foot wall. And he had no way of finding out. Simon had to keep himself pinned in his snow seat to prevent being yanked off the face by the hanging dead weight of Joe. And there they stayed for nearly an hour, one man helplessly hanging, the other helplessly bracing against the constant pull, each growing increasingly tired, cold, and discouraged in the night.

Joe bounced down a few inches, then a few more, then a few more. He knew what was happening. What a shame for it to end like this. Joe knew at any moment that Simon would be yanked off the mountain. Certain death for both of them. He waited.

Suddenly he was falling. The rope whipped against his face as he accelerated and smashed through the roof of the crevasse. He accelerated again until he jolted to an abrupt stop in the dark stillness. His wind was gone as was all sense of time as he lay in a dreamy state. The cold air and pain in his leg eventually revived him. Miraculously, he had survived the 100-plus-foot fall, and he laughed till he cried, the laugh of a fool. But what had stopped him?

In the darkness he reached and felt a wall of ice. He continued the sweep of his arm and felt it suddenly drop into space. He was on a ledge or bridge, but he didn't know where to move to secure his position. He hammered an ice screw into the wall and clipped into it. At least he was secure—alone in the night in the dark silence of a crevasse high in the Peruvian Andes, badly injured, cold, without food or water, completely unaware of his situation or what he could do—but secure.

The hope that had begun to build as the two had moved down the face was nearly gone. People who fall into crevasses die in them. The rope, still attached to his harness on one end, disappeared back up through the top of the crevasse. He tugged, hoping to find resistance, hoping it was somehow anchored above so he could pull himself up. He pulled, and the rope came easily until it fell limply near him. He pulled the end to him. It had been cut. Once Simon began to be pulled off the mountain, he made the decision that climbers who are roped together often don't have time to make—he cut the rope. Had their circumstances been reversed, Joe would have done the same thing.

The long night passed in the crevasse. It was nearly dawn, and Joe began shouting Simon's name. Futilely. Certain that Joe was dead, Simon had left. Considering the circumstances, it was the only reasonable conclusion he could have come to.

Joe couldn't climb up. His simple choices were to stay on the ice bridge and wait for a cold, dark, slow, and solitary death or to descend even farther into the crevasse, hoping to reach the bottom and maybe find a way out. Once he began his attempt, there would be no turning back. Forty feet or 400—he had no way of knowing if he would run out of rope long before he reached the bottom. And he had no way of knowing if the bottom offered a solution or merely a deeper tomb.

He began his rappel of faith by lowering himself down the bridge away from the ice screw for 50 feet. His legs suddenly dropped free into open space, and he stopped the descent, gripping the rope and its illusion of safety. He was well beyond the point of no return, but there was still something unnerving about the sudden drop. He eased his grip and continued. For 20 feet he fought the desire to look down. If he saw a floor, he would know he'd made the right decision. But if he saw only more black…

Finally he looked and saw the bottom, only 15 feet away. Once on the floor, he looked around, hoping but not expecting to find a way out. Forty feet away he saw a cone of snow and ice, 15 feet at the bottom, tapering to a top of 4 feet, angling up 130 feet, all the way to the ceiling. Joe judged its angle to be forty-five degrees for most of the way, sixty-five nearer the top. A ten-minute climb for someone with two good legs. Climbable at all in his condition? He would find out soon enough. He now had a way to escape the despair and darkness of the crevasse. A narrow, gold pillar of sunlight pierced the roof, a symbol of promise and hope.

"The change in me was astonishing. I felt invigorated, full of energy and optimism. I could see possible dangers, very real risks that could destroy my hopes, but somehow I knew I could overcome them. It was as if I had been given this one blessed chance to get out and I was grasping it with every ounce of strength left in me." He began to climb, awkwardly at first. He dug his ice axes into the column and pulled with his arms. It wouldn't work on the steeper section, and he was vulnerable to a fall even at the bottom if one of his axes ripped free. He needed a better system.

Joe reached down with an ax and chopped a step into the cone. He tamped it down, then reached a little farther and chopped a smaller step. He then planted his axes into the snow above, brought his bad leg up onto the small step for balance, hopped with his good leg, and pressed his arms down for extra thrust. The pain shot through his leg but soon faded. It had worked. Once again he dug the steps, planted his axes, and thrust up. And on it continued for two and a half hours as he climbed up the first 80 feet of the cone. The angle increased as did the risk and potential consequences of a failed step. Another two and a half hours had him exhausted but within 10 feet of the ceiling. He resumed his planting-and-hopping climb until his head poked through the roof, and he hauled himself into the sunlight.

He'd escaped the awful darkness of the crevasse, and he lay motionless in the snow as waves of relief and exhaustion rolled over him. The sun warmed him, and he vaguely registered the spectacular scenery and the feeling of freedom. In spite of his escape and the relief he now felt, an awareness of his circumstances slowly rose in his mind: six miles from their base camp with no food or water. Though anxious about what lay ahead, he had long ago come to terms with the likelihood of his death. At least he would die in a struggle for life. And so he rose, planted his ice axes in the snow, and began hopping toward the glacier 200 feet away.

Once he reached the icy glacier, he immediately fell headlong. The hop he had perfected was useless on the new surface. Okay, crawl it is. At least he had found Simon's footprints in the snow, giving him an essential trail to safely follow across the glacier and a welcome sense of companionship. He quickly learned the least painful way to crawl. Lying on his left side, pulling with his ice axes while shoving with his good leg, he began making steady progress. Plant, pull, shove. Plant, pull, shove. He occasionally lost himself in an exhausted daydream but would be awakened by what seemed to be a voice urging him on. He would resume the plant-pull-shove tracing of Simon's trail.

And then a late-afternoon storm arrived, its falling temperatures accompanied by wind and snow that quickly began to obscure Simon's prints. He continued to crawl well into the stormy night until he crawled over a bank of snow. It was a perfect spot to dig a snow cave, and he did. Eventually his pain, fears, and frustration were overcome by exhaustion, and he fell asleep.

He began his second day of complete isolation painfully, his body having tightened with the injury and a cramped night of inactivity. As he glanced around the glacier, he saw that it was covered with a thick, soft, formless blanket of snow. The trail and any signs of the treacherous crevasses that lay just below the surface were now completely obscured. It was his third day without food or water. The snow he could melt in his mouth couldn't possibly meet his body's demands for water, given the altitude and level of exertion.

His tongue was thick and dry. It stuck to the roof of his mouth. He smelled water in the snow around him, driving him to a near panic. Once again he began his crawl, more carefully now as there were no tracks to follow. He attempted to walk, a decision that immediately proved to be agonizingly wrong as he fell, the bones in his shattered knee once again grating and twisting.

While standing, he had seen the beginnings of a complex section of crevasses he remembered navigating with Simon on their way in. It had been a challenge for the two of them while fresh and able to walk. They had taken mental notes to make their return trip easier. Joe recognized the near impossibility of making it through alive. Had there been an alternative other than the certain death of inactivity, he would have taken it. But he could come up with none, so he began his dangerous crawl.

"It was impossible to judge where I was in relation to the vague map in my mind. I would recognize a crevasse, then look again and see that I was mistaken. Each one changed shape when I glanced at it a second time, and my head was swimming with the effort of concentration. A mounting horror of falling into a crevasse forced me into frantic guessing at the best path through the maze. The harder I tried, the worse my position became, until hysteria threatened to overwhelm me. Which way, which way?" He crawled, then doubled back on himself, looking for a way out of the craziness.

Then something clicked as he approached a snow bridge spanning two open holes. He'd already dismissed the bridge several times before, but the feeling was strong enough this time that he chanced standing to confirm his suspicions. He recognized the bridge as the way out and crawled to relative safety. As he paused to celebrate his good fortune and progress, he noticed a difficulty focusing on either what lay before him or the section of crevasses he had just come through. He rubbed his eyes and it got worse. Snow blindness. He'd have to attempt the moraines, a dangerous section of boulders, rocks, and glacial debris just ahead, while squinting through narrow slits of eyes.

Joe quickly learned that however painfully difficult his crawl across the glacier had been, it had been easy compared to the hopping he would have to do to cross the uneven boulder-and-rock field. He fashioned a crude splint from his sleeping mat and began to hop. He immediately fell, twisting his knee and hitting his head on a boulder. He rose, managed a half step, then fell again. And on it went for a painful ten yards—successful small step, fall on the next. But he perfected his hop. The pain alternated between a dull pulse and agonizing stabs on the inevitable falls, but he hopped on.

He had learned the importance of timing his progress. Instead of focusing on getting all the way back to camp, he would see a landmark in the distance and set a goal of reaching it in thirty minutes. The snow he could melt in his mouth had always been a dangerously insufficient source of water, and now whatever snow remained was becoming full of dirt and grit.

He stumbled on, well into the dark of evening, licking the mud for water when he fell, ignoring the voice that kept imploring him to stop and sleep. He fell once again but could not lift himself this time. He crawled into his sleeping bag at 10:00 p.m., ending his second full day of complete isolation.

Joe awakened the next morning cold, stiff, exhausted. He'd hit a wall. Mental? Physical? Probably both. Too weak to move or care. He wanted to lift his arm to shield his eyes from the sun's glare, but he couldn't. He lay there, still and scared.

He knew this would be his last chance to make base camp. Simon would have recovered enough from the exertion of the climb and descent to leave. Certain that Joe was dead, there would be no reason for him to stay. For the first time he faced the idea that he could return to base camp only to find there would be no base camp. The thought spurred him to action. Eight o'clock, ten hours of daylight ahead. He stepped, fell, then rose, again and again and again.

Each fall brought a furious debate—to quit or to continue. To stay down or to get up. With each fall, the combined power of days of isolation, pain, frustration, fear, and exhaustion hammered at his will to survive. Continue his painful pursuit of an uncertain goal or to abandon himself to an easy death? Each time he lifted himself, his will triumphed. He desperately wanted to quit, to drift into a haze where the dehydration, exhaustion, starvation, and pain could not reach him. Free from the torment of any thoughts of surviving, he could slide peacefully into unconsciousness until death claimed him. But his mind was set. From the moment he had emerged from the crevasse, he knew he would keep moving by whatever scoot/hop/crawl means he could.

By 1:00 p.m. he'd reached a trickling supply of water. He gulped with the mindless abandon of an animal, quenching the burning in his throat, but not his thirst. He gulped and gulped and felt his strength returning.

He began to look around and recognized the surroundings. They had been there eight days before. A lifetime ago, and yet it seemed like only yesterday. He still didn't know if there was a camp. Revived by the water and a hope that he was close, he again set off. "It felt so normal to hurt that I was no longer surprised by the torment which ambushed me with every fall," he said. He shuffled, hopped, fell, slipped into dreamy periods of inactivity, then began again. He was reduced to leaning heavily on his ax in a bent-over crouch and eventually to crawling on his belly. Additional recognizable landmarks came into view and were eventually overtaken. Once again a late afternoon storm descended, the winds bringing freezing rain first, then snow. As he crawled, he felt a rising fear, not of falling this time, but of finding that Simon and Richard had broken camp, leaving him abandoned again, fatally this time. He crawled blindly into the night, battling fatigue and delirium, guided only by an instinctive sense of which way he ought to proceed.

He pulled himself up onto a boulder. It was nearly 1:00 a.m., and as he blankly stared into the darkness, he was startled to a new, if still confused, level of alertness by the foul stench of excrement. He slowly realized he was in what had been their camp's latrine area. But was there still a camp? He shouted as best he could and waited. Nothing.

"Siiiiiiimon...," he repeated.

"The night remained black," he says. "I wanted it to end. I felt destroyed. For the first time in many days, I accepted that I had finally come to the end of my strength. I needed someone, anyone. "Help meeeeeeee!"

At first he thought the hazy glows of light he saw in the distance might be spaceships—hallucinations. He'd certainly had them before. Then he heard muffled sounds and voices. Then more light and discernable movement.

"Joe! Is that you? Joe!" exclaimed Simon.

He'd made it. The return that seemed impossible wasn't. The base camp he wasn't sure still existed did. In spite of a crippling injury, frostbite, no food or water, exposure to hostile weather, exhaustion, the immeasurable toll of eight days of climbing, sliding, crawling, falling, and an overwhelming sense of complete isolation, he had made it. It's one of extreme sports' greatest survival stories. It's also one of history's greatest examples of step-by-step, moment-by-moment, decision-by-decision, action-by-action faith. Certain of what he hoped for, sure of what he could not see, he pressed on.

## MIDLIFE AND MARRIAGE

A married couple can be progressing through life—the months and years passing in a blur of establishing a home, raising a family, and building a career or two. Then something happens that disrupts the steady march. It could be an event. The death or serious illness of a peer or family member may make the uncertainties of life painfully apparent. The departure of a child for college may awaken you to the sudden passing of eighteen years of your life.

A business failure may cause a financial reversal that shows with painful clarity where your sense of worth really comes from. Or another business success may reinforce a sense of bored compla-cency. The breakup of the marriage of friends you thought you knew, a couple with whom you seemed to share so much, may make you suddenly suspicious of what goes on beneath the surface, including your own surface.

It could be as subtle as a fortieth birthday that starts you think-ing as never before about regrets over the past, concerns about the future, and restlessness about the present. What used to work for you (whatever that means), both personally and professionally, may no longer work as well, if at all. The emphasis of our culture stays stubbornly stuck on youth and beauty, but you are irreversibly moving on. Your hair is grayer than it used to be, maybe thinner, too. You may be heavier than you should be. And you feel much more confined by relationships and circumstances than you want to be.

Perhaps you notice that you can't sustain the same level of physical effort for as long. Maybe for the first time in your life you need reading glasses. You're aware of little aches and pains—nothing to be concerned about except that you can't connect them with a cause, unless you go way, way back to that fall, that accident, or that time in high school when you rolled your ankle. The evidence mounts that the years are piling up.

The summit in life you thought you'd attained or knew you were pushing for may be suddenly up for grabs. You may feel trapped by the very different needs and expectations of two generations, your children behind you and your aging parents ahead of you. The work you do, whether it is in the marketplace or your family, may seem meaningless and mundane.

The intensity and adventurousness of your sexual relationship may have lapsed into a predictable progression. You may feel like your marriage is a bleak place of routine and frustrated expectations. You know you need a change and may believe that the biggest obstacle to a different life is your spouse. You wonder how you got where you are, but then knowing what you know now, you conclude it couldn't have worked out any differently. You may shake your head at the naiveté of your earlier feelings of excited love yet still crave excitement and connection.

There's a time of reevaluation in the lives of many people in their middle thirties to early forties. It's such a common occurrence that we've given it a name. And it's such a significant, potentially threatening time that, just like sex and death, we try to disarm it with clever slang and cliché images. It's commonly called a midlife crisis.

In spite of the fact that many people aren't aware of it or don't admit to it, it is real and has enormous potential. Whether it is a constructive, purposeful midlife transition or destructive, flailing midlife crisis will depend greatly on how well a person has done the life work we have been discussing all along.

## Life Reassessment

"Reassessment is the prevailing theme of the midlife," says Jim Conway. The person in midlife is full of questions. "Is this all there is? What should I have done differently? Has my chance passed me by? Does my work have any meaning? Does my life have any meaning? Does anybody really know me? Do I really know me? Am I making a difference? Am I making a difference in my kids' lives? Do my friends really like me, or are my relationships just a matter of habit and convenience? Why did I marry this person? Is my marriage worth it? Why am I feeling this way? Why am I not happy or satisfied or… Will I ever be?" If these questions sound familiar, it's because some of them are the same as those asked by teenagers in adolescence.

If you've not embraced the goal of Christlikeness and determined specifically what that means in your life, you could be in big trouble. Your sense of entitlement may be aroused as never before, and because of social skills and financial resources, you may be able to gratify it as never before. You may reject the ideal of serving one another in love and wonder when it's your turn to just relax and enjoy. You've got a lot of catching up to do. And instead of rising purposefully from disappointments in your life and marriage, you cycle back into entitlement.

If you've never done the work of self-discovery, you may not even be able to explain the restlessness, frustration, and irritability you're feeling. But you feel those things and more. It's very possible that because of your own fear or the perceived limitations of the roles you've assumed, you've spent much of your life suppressing key aspects of who God made you to be or choosing not to express them. But they keep popping up, very likely with greater strength and frequency. You're not happy, and you know you need to change things, but you don't know what to change or how.

If you've never accepted responsibility for your own attitudes, feelings, and actions, there's always your spouse to blame. Or your job. Or your family of origin. That's easy. Counterproductive and certain to keep you from growing, but easy.

If you've never invested the time in developing friendships or taken the risks to develop deep friendships, the lack of connection you feel in your marriage may be further compounded by the lack of friends who know you, accept you, and can speak "the truth in love" to you (Ephesians 4:15).

If you've never admitted how necessary physical and emotional faithfulness are to the survival of your marriage and the well-being of your soul, you may begin to develop relationships that are dangerously, perhaps fatally, disorienting. Short-term feel-good solutions may seem surprisingly attractive, even justifiable, regardless of potential long-term destructive consequences.

If you've never chosen to focus on discovering and understanding your spouse's needs and expectations, it's possible you'll see him or her as an impossible-to-satisfy drain on your time and energy or, worse, an obstacle that stands between you and happiness.

If you've not purposefully built into your mate and your marriage, he or she may feel like a guard that's checking up on you, and your marriage may seem like a prison that confines you.

## A Critical Choice

From the moment Joe Simpson roused himself to awareness on the ice bridge in the crevasse, he had a decision to make. Was he going to die alone or stubbornly struggle to return to what he knew was once there and what he hoped could still be?

Eventually people's lives will bring them to a point of choice, and they will face three alternatives. First, they can keep going straight ahead, doing the same things they have always done, going through the motions, neither completely investing in nor completely abandoning the relationship. The path they are on, however dull or disappointing, is easier than mustering the energy to change and grow. This indifference is death to a successful marriage.

Second, they can decide to change, and change for most people means changing their external circumstances. They may change jobs. They may change friends. They may change their weight, their hair, their car, their activities, maybe even change what they believe about God. And they may change their marital status by pursuing a divorce or allowing one to happen. This kind of emotional abandonment is death.

Or, third, they can change themselves from the inside out. Discomfort can be a great catalyst for growth. It might be due to a new urgency that comes with the ticking clock of life or the accumulation of wisdom to know and courage to do, but midlife has a way of showing people the things they really need to work on. They can do the tough work of purposeful, God-honoring growth. With the help of their climbing partner, they can figure out fresh ways to honor existing commitments in the continued pursuit of Christlikeness. They can make the relationship more rewarding and satisfying for both of them. They can pursue a new relationship with the same person.

A person who chooses this inside-out growth will face all those familiar obstacles and distractions. Extreme marriages don't just work out. They are something you plan for and relentlessly pursue. But even then, many marriages won't survive the challenges of midlife if a successful marriage is your primary goal. The price of a successful marriage is huge, more than many people are willing to pay. After years of trying, some people conclude that the costs they are paying far exceed the benefits they are receiving, that the risks they are taking outweigh the rewards they are experiencing.

At times I've done that worldly cost-benefit analysis. And at times I've come to the conclusion that the price I'm paying is exceeding the benefits I'm receiving. Tari has too. At times my risks have been greater than my rewards. Same with Tari. And at different times we have both been right—if we focused on immediate relational rewards. But we have persevered.

In Hebrews 11:1, Paul defined faith as "being sure of what we hope for and certain of what we do not see." Tari and I are both sure of the kind of relationship we hope for and the people we hope to be. And we are certain of Jesus's character, even if we do not see it completed in either ourselves or each other. It is the unique lens of marriage that allows us to see, sometimes with disappointing clarity, our spouse's imperfections. And our own.

So we follow Paul's simple formula in Philippians 3:13–14: "Forgetting what is behind and straining toward what is ahead," we press on. Sometimes we climb with strength and grace. Sometimes we limp along. Sometimes we crawl. Sometimes it is only the promise of what can be that gives each of us the strength we need to press on. To quit on marriage is to quit on the process of becoming like Jesus. Marriage is Plan A. There is no Plan B.

If you see marriage as an invaluable tool in transforming your character more completely into something like Jesus's character, then no price is too high. Even if it hurts. Even if you think the emptiness may never end but would be relieved if it did. Even if you don't know if you can make it back or if there is a "back" to return to. You will climb, crawl, scramble, and hop—whatever it takes—because you recognize the person you are becoming is worth the price you are paying. And in the process, you can attain the marriage you hope for.

## Summary

Don't be surprised if you or your spouse begins to feel a sort of restlessness about life in general, or your marriage specifically, in your late thirties. The best way to prepare for what might happen then is to build a relationship foundation now, one that is strong enough to withstand the unexpected shocks of life but flexible enough to absorb change. When it comes, if it comes, do whatever it takes to continue your pursuit of the characteristics you have seen in Jesus. Make it a purposeful, constructive transition, not a desperate, destructive change.

## For Reflection

1. What two things would each of you like to have said you'd accomplished before you reach the age of sixty?
2. What area of talent or giftedness do you see in your spouse that is not being fully utilized?

# They Told You About the Guano, Right?

## Exploring Each Other and Yourself is Like Caving

> *But for the true explorer—the carrier of that uniquely*
> *human gene that drives her or him to proclaim,*
> *I must be the first one there—the ever shrinking planet*
> *offers only one remaining option: look underground*
> *where not even the satellites can reach.*
>
> MICHAEL RAY TAYLOR, caver

T he only thing we have to fear is fear itself—nameless, unreasoning, unjustified terror, which paralyzes needed efforts to convert retreat into advance." Franklin Roosevelt said those words at his inauguration as the thirty-second president of the United States, the occasion apparently sort of a pep rally for phobophobes—people with a fear of fear. FDR may have battled polio and led our nation through the Great Depression and virtually all of World War II, but obviously he had never been caving.

Caving has a fear for everyone. Are you a hygrophobe, someone with a fear of moisture? The humidity in most caves is nearly 100 percent, always. Or maybe moisture of a more direct kind, like water, is your fear. That would make you a hydrophobe. Nothing like plunging up to your chin into refreshingly cool, fifty-five-degree water to exacerbate your concerns and maybe bring on a case of hypothermia. If the thought of crab-walking with an oozing, mucous-like mud sucking at your boots and gloves makes you think that caving might not be the sport for you, you might be a blenno-phobe, someone who is afraid of slime.

If you struggle with nyctophobia, a fear of darkness, stay out of caves. You could easily find yourself in a turning, narrow, rocky pas-sageway a few hundred feet from even a sliver of sunlight. Nothing swallows light like a cave. There is no dark like cave dark, and there is no quiet like cave quiet. If you stopped to think about it, which you probably shouldn't, a cave is as dark and quiet as a tomb. And speaking of tombs, if you're taphophobic, it would be reasonable to assume that your fear of being buried alive might be activated a hun-dred feet or more beneath the earth's surface.

There is a general guideline in caving that if your upturned boot can fit through an opening, so can you, at least physically. If your boot size is eleven, that gives you about twelve inches. Now whether or not your psyche can handle crawling across a hundred feet of rock on your elbows, stomach, and knees, with your helmet scraping the top of the twelve-inch crawlway is another story. Claustrophobia is a fear of confined spaces, and in a cave you are certain to acquire a new appreciation for the old saying "between a rock and a hard place." And though it almost certainly wouldn't happen, you can't help but wonder if you are but one seismic hiccup away from becoming a permanent subterranean hyphen, just one panic attack from becoming helplessly wedged in some unyielding passage with a name like the Birth Canal and eventually becoming a sort of buffet line for the bats and sightless troglobites that live there.

There's actually some misinformation about bats and caves. No, they don't attack people, get into their hair, or try to suck their blood. They leave people alone and would prefer to be left alone. And though they do prefer the stable, cool, damp darkness of caves, you could go all the way through a cave and not see a bat. So any stories you've heard about cavers tramping through bat guano might be the exaggerations of eager storytellers. On the other hand, they could be talking about Bracken Cave in Texas, home to an estimated twenty million bats who leave each night in search of insects to eat.

Actually, fear and phobia are not the same thing. Fear is an "emotion of alarm or agitation caused by the expectation or realization of danger." Fear is rational. Fear can be prudent. Fear is simply a warning signal that you're physically or emotionally at risk. A phobia is fear ratcheted up to an irrational, illogical, excessive level. It is disproportionate to the situation and accompanied by avoidance of the situation. It is more about you than the dilemma you face. People on the outside looking in can't figure out why you're terrified of flying or clowns or thunder.

Perhaps more than any other extreme sport, caving requires a mastery of fear. Generally it's not fast enough to demand your attention the way snowboarding and whitewater kayaking do, for example, so you have time to think. If you choose to think about your fears, you'll have a short career as a caver. Caving is a head game, from start to finish. Either you master your fears, or your fears master you.

How do caves form? It's a simple process. A little water, a table of soluble rock with some vertical fissures, more than a few years—next thing you know, Mammoth Cave, which is the world's largest known cave system with more than 350 miles of mapped passageways.

Most of the caves in the United States have been formed in vast beds of limestone. Geologists say that at one time much of what is now dry land was actually the floor of a shallow sea. Through time, deposits of rock, sand, silt, dead fish, and shellfish collected in different layers. Eventually, the geologists say, the seas dried up, leaving behind the various strata of rock. And then what we know as soil and plants covered the limestone beds so they looked more like prairies than sea floors. Somewhere along the line, natural occurrences like earthquakes caused massive shifts in the rock, resulting in vertical fissures.

Rain and snowmelt accumulated in slight depressions on the surface. That water soaked into the soil, picking up carbon dioxide and becoming a mild solution of carbonic acid, much like a carbonated beverage. The acid naturally followed the path of least resistance to the lowest point it could find—those vertical cracks. As the acid flowed into the cracks, it imperceptibly dissolved the walls, making them microscopically wider. Eventually this water found a horizontal weakness in the layers, maybe even a gap, and it began its sideways motion. This is a long process, very long. But as the fissures and gaps enlarged, more water entered, and the process accelerated.

Before you know it, raging underground rivers were carving out enormous caverns beneath the earth's surface. And then the water table lowered to the point where the passage was no longer a raging river. It flowed rather than raged. Eventually it became a babbling brook or just a section of standing water in an otherwise dry cave—ready for exploration.

Getting around in a cave is obviously different from moving around on the surface. In a cave you go where a passage takes you, and you rarely know where it's taking you until you're there. A caver is intentional about exploration. He is trying to get deeper or farther and understands that many passages will dead-end, in spite of the last hour he has spent walking, then scrambling, then crawling on his stomach in exploration. Of course, a passage could also be the one that other cavers have chosen not to go down or overlooked altogether that opens into an enormous cavern, like the one discovered by caving legend Marion Smith in 2000.

One day in early 1997, Fred Hutchison, an acquaintance of Smith's, discovered a cave entrance that went a few feet, then dropped into a pit. He came back another day for some more serious exploring that included a sixty-eight-foot rappel into the pit, a five-hundred-foot walk up a stream, up one waterfall, then another fifty feet to the base of a second. He judged the fourteen-foot falls too difficult to climb and turned back.

Hutchinson registered the location and filed a name, Rumbling Falls, with the local caving organization. With no apparent interest in exploring farther, he did not object when Smith approached him in 1998 about the possibility of continuing the exploration himself. Smith and a team of cavers began their work in September.

They agreed it would be a project they would map as they went. They would share the tedium of mapping as well as the fun of discovery. It's not just *important* to be observant in a cave; it is absolutely *essential*. Cavers can only see what they illuminate, and they remember only what they make it a point to remember. So they develop keen powers of observation. They frequently look over their shoulders to note where they've come from, because it will look different on the way back, perhaps much different. They stop and look around at intersections and are constantly noting other passageways, ground formations, and features and striations on the walls and ceiling. Because you might walk an easy mile in a cave quicker than you crawl a challenging hundred feet, distance can be very deceptive.

Observational skills are critical for survival. Mapping skills are essential for ongoing exploration. Depending on the size and complexity of the cave, mapping it can take years of exploration, so you need to be able to return to where you left off. The tools for mapping are a measuring tape, a compass, and a device for measuring incline called a clinometer. A cave cartographer is not only noting distance and incline, he is also measuring the height and width of the passage.

Because you're moving in the dark through existing networks of rigid passages that are as likely to dead-end as they are to continue, mapping is a process of trial and error that requires patience, diligence, and courage. But the cave will give you many clues, if you know what you're looking for.

"The best way to begin to find new passages within a known cave is to understand its geologic nature," says Michael Ray Taylor in his book *Caves: Exploring Hidden Realms.* "Does it follow a particular fault or ridge? Is it related to surface topography? Does an ancient drainage pattern govern the major passageways?"

By their fourth visit to the cave, Smith's team had proceeded more than two thousand feet into the side of the hill, far beyond the second waterfall that had deterred Hutchison. Smith was leading when he came to a hole "the size of an office wastebasket." He squeezed through, turned a corner, and came onto a ledge.

If you've never been in the dark silence of a wild cave (undeveloped, in its natural state, without the lighting and paths of a commercialized cave), you can't really appreciate what Smith encountered. After beginning each expedition with a familiar sixty-eight-foot rappel into the pit, followed by nearly a half mile of moving through a well-defined passageway, his light shot out into "a vast expanse of blackness." He knew his cave had just changed, but it took a while to figure out just how dramatic the change was.

"Smith tossed a rock off the lip. It fell silently for what seemed a very long time before exploding at the bottom," says Taylor. "The sound rumbled across the floor of an enormous chamber." It was more than two hundred feet to the floor, which was littered with car-sized boulders. As the team investigated, they discovered the walls angled away from the wide, flat top, forming a volcano-shaped cavern large enough to contain the Louisiana Superdome. The Superdome, home to the NFL's New Orleans Saints and site of six Super Bowls, can accommodate seventy-two thousand people in its stands. The name given to Smith's discovery, Stupendous Pit, was no exaggeration. But the exploration didn't stop there. Over the months that followed, the team continued exploring and mapping for miles, discovering one chamber about 370 by 150 feet with a ceiling 120 feet high, and another 800 feet long and 200 feet wide.

Like all extreme sports, caving is a physically dangerous sport best left to people who approach it with the respect it deserves. In addition to the danger, the environment deserves enormous respect. Unfortunately, in a topside world of instant gratification, planned obsolescence, and spare parts, a deep and abiding respect for the creative process and resulting creation can be hard to come by.

Serious cavers are often tight lipped about their explorations. They know that they are the ones who will have to rescue the inexperienced novices and unprepared thrill seekers who head into caves without appropriate regard for the danger or the environment. In their eagerness to get into the cave, novices sometimes forget to carefully note how they will get back out and sometimes get lost underground.

The thrill seekers drop their only flashlight, or their only battery dies. They sit and await rescue or stumble around in the dark, either getting more lost or, if they're lucky, finding their way out. They damage the interior by leaving behind beer cans, food wrappers, and graffiti that those more respectful of the environment will have to clean up. Or they could damage or destroy a cave formation that has been forming for thousands of years. Whether out of carelessness, ignorance, or disregard, the damage is done.

## Exploring Another's Soul and Your Own

Marriage should also be left to people who respect the danger and the environment and who regard the process of soul exploration as a sacred trust. The more you discover, the greater your responsibility to love and respect your spouse. And as you discover more about your spouse, you'll be discovering more about yourself as well. You will learn about your capacities to love, honor, and accept your mate. Each of you and the unique oneness of your marriage are examples of God's creative work. Your carelessness or direct attempts to change what is unchangeable in either you or your spouse could badly damage both of you and destroy the relationship.

Some of what you will find out about each other in marriage is the junk left behind by other relationships that have preceded you. Could be family. Could be friends. Could be romantic relationships. You can get to some pretty risky places, for both the person exploring and the one being explored. Previous imperfect relationships with imperfect people may have resulted in some garbage left behind, stuff that's now part of the emotional and psychological makeup of you and your spouse. Remembering that Christlikeness is your goal, you get to help with a little soul cleanup of yourself and each other. It's part of the marriage deal.

Unfortunately, marriage is often undertaken by novices who don't have the knowledge to recognize and appreciate the unique features of another's soul, the skills to survive, the courage to persevere, or the patience to develop those qualities. They get scared or frustrated and fall back into some old pattern of protecting themselves. It's also entered into by those looking for some near-desperate way to meet their God-given desire for connection, even if the only skills they have are short-term and self-centered.

One of the first things we have to do in marriage is create an environment of courageous acceptance of the person. It is not a one-time deal. As life progresses and your relationship grows, you will find out new things about your spouse and yourself. Some will delight you and some will alarm you. Some will be discovered, and others you'll choose to reveal. You may stumble across attitudes or behaviors you cannot accept, but you reject those, not the person. You need to continue to build the environment of acceptance. It's a way of life, not an event.

Sometimes your most important discoveries in marriage come just beyond the most challenging section—the tight crawlway of a repeated area of conflict, the blind rappel into the dark and unexpected hole of some addiction or compulsive behavior, the passageway that is flooded up to your chin with glib behavior that hides an embarrassing shortcoming. These are the sections you and others may have chosen to bypass or where you may have turned back before. They could be passageways in yourself or your spouse.

If you choose to explore these sections and make it through, you might find formations of awesome strength and staggering beauty, but you could also find vast caverns of pain and emptiness. Either way, if together you muster the faith and courage to continue, your connectedness can grow, and the bond will become more secure.

What will you discover in marriage? Hopefully you began with a clear understanding of your personality and that of your partner, how each of you was created. Regardless of how life experiences have shaped or misshaped your personality or how you may have assumed roles that suppressed it, there is an unalterable core of who you are. To try to fundamentally change yours or your spouse's is to damage or even destroy it. It is disrespectful.

Understanding who we are and what specific gifts we have provides important clues in this process of exploring one another. As life and marriage go on, one thing we should try to accomplish is to bring what we do on a day-to-day basis more in line with who we are. We should do it for ourselves, for our spouse, and for our children. It's a much more efficient use of our emotional energy, and it will take us much nearer the goal of Christlikeness that we have been pursuing all along. It can be a long process, and some aspects of development may have to be sacrificed in the short term in order to achieve a larger goal.

One of the great things about an extreme marriage is that because we know each other, we don't get spooked by the unknown or the unexpected. We can look back and understand where we have been as individuals and as a couple. We are secure in where we are, even if it is not where we want to be. We can look ahead in the cave and know where we want to go, in spite of the fact that we can see only as far ahead as our light can illuminate. It will continue to be a process of trial and error and discovery, but we're getting better at reading the geological clues.

Since we have the base knowledge of personality, family of origin, and significant life experiences, we can look ahead to hopes and dreams, the ideas and passions and gifts that God has entrusted to each of us. An aspiration could be as large and public as Mel Gibson's movie *The Passion of the Christ* or as small and private, but no less significant, as a passion to be an outstanding parent. They could be as short-term as this year or as big-picture as the epitaph on your headstone.

Regardless of how public or private, big or small, short-term or long-term they are, the important thing is that we have hopes and dreams, that we share them with one another, and that we pursue them together—even if that means only to give genuine support.

## A Spirit of Exploration

If you started your wedding ceremony by putting on a jumpsuit and stepping out of a plane, you should bring along your coveralls, helmet, gloves, and boots to change into after the reception. Three sources of light and spare batteries would be an excellent idea too. You don't know what you're going to find in the passageways of marriage or when you're going to find it.

It's going to be the hardest work you've ever done. It will require more courage than you knew you had. It will demand a spirit of adventure and curiosity that is never satisfied. It will take you places you never knew existed, places you thought you'd never have to go to, and places you hope you never have to go back to. Unlike most caves, you'll certainly have to deal with some guano in your marriage. But hey, it's great fertilizer—kind of an "all things work together for good" deal (Romans 8:28, KJV).

But it will also take you to places of sheer strength and fragile beauty, of beautifully striated walls and cleverly sculpted formations, of wide-eyed discovery and ever-reaching mystery. Places you'll hate to leave and can't wait to get back to. It's a lot of little discoveries and disappointments along the way to the big discoveries.

Relationship is to our souls what water is to a cave—a creative force of both awesome power and intricate craftsmanship. And no earthly relationship has the potential to be as powerful or intricate as marriage. As long as there is relationship, the process of creation continues within us.

If you stick with it, the two of you can progressively become a more intimately connected one. Your marriage adventure will take you deeper into yourself and your spouse, to places where you understand as never before the idea of "fearfully and wonderfully made"

(Psalm 139:14). You will know that "perfect love drives out fear" (1 John 4:18), and even though you love imperfectly and always will, you also love with increasing courage, steadfastness, and purpose.

That's an extreme marriage.

## Summary

Marriage. The great adventure. The great exploration. You don't know what you've gotten yourself into. There's probably a parenthood passage somewhere further into the cave. But you don't know exactly where it is, nor do you know what you'll find there, either in yourself or your spouse. You know there's a health passage in there too. It could be in thirty years, or it could be next week. It could be you, your mate, your children, your parents. Who knows? And who knows what you'll discover about everyone involved? There's at least a dozen fill-in-the-blank passages ahead. Who knows about any of this stuff? Don't be afraid of the unknown, because there's a lot of it in your future.

## For Reflection

1. Since you've been married or seriously dating, what two discoveries have you made about the other person that most encourage you about your future together?

2. Since you've been married or seriously dating, what one discovery have you made about yourself that most concerns you about your future together?

A small group discussion guide
on the topics covered in *Extreme Marriage*
is available free of charge
at www.waterbrookpress.com.

# notes

## Chapter 1: The Most Extreme of Them All
*page*

5 The epigraph to this chapter is drawn from Mark Jenkins, *The Hard Way* (New York: Simon & Schuster, 2002), 206.

11–12 *Tanya Streeter record:* Redefine Your Limits, www.redefineyour limits.com.

12 *"By nature, we":* Lawrence J. Crabb, *Understanding Who You Are: What Your Relationships Tell You About Yourself* (Colorado Springs: NavPress, 1997), 10.

*"What marriage has done for me":* Gary Thomas, *Sacred Marriage: What If God Designed Marriage to Make Us Holy More Than to Make Us Happy?* (Grand Rapids: Zondervan, 2000), 93.

12–13 *"Sometimes what is hard…never experienced before":* Thomas N. Hart and Kathleen Fischer Hart, *The First Two Years of Marriage: Foundations for a Life Together* (New York: Paulist Press, 1983), 50, quoted in Thomas, *Sacred Marriage,* 93.

15 *"When you see 'Christianity' read":* Don Everts, *Jesus with Dirty Feet: A Down-to-Earth Look at Christianity for the Curious & Skeptical* (Downers Grove, IL: InterVarsity Press, 1999), 20.

## Chapter 2: The Greatest Race You Never Heard Of
*page*

17 The epigraph to this chapter is drawn from Martin Dugard, *Surviving the Toughest Race on Earth* (New York: McGraw-Hill, 1998), 107.

20 *Adventure walking in sand, snow:* Liz Caldwell and Barry Siff, *Adventure Racing: The Ultimate Guide* (Boulder, CO: VeloPress, 2001), 60.

23 *"More team disagreements, arguments":* Caldwell and Siff, *Adventure Racing,* 99.

24    *definition of* con petire: Mihaly Csikszentmihalyi and Susan A. Jackson, *Flow in Sports: The Keys to Optimal Experiences and Performances* (Champaign, IL: Human Kinetics, 1999), 80.

*"Everyone's personality will be amplified during a race"*: Caldwell and Siff, *Adventure Racing,* 31.

25    *"What if God designed marriage to make us holy"*: Gary Thomas, *Sacred Marriage: What If God Designed Marriage to Make Us Holy More Than to Make Us Happy?* (Grand Rapids: Zondervan, 2000), 13.

26    *"The worst value ever"*: Henry Cloud and John Townsend, *Boundaries in Marriage* (Grand Rapids: Zondervan, 1999), 108.

*"The reason is that happiness is a result"*: Cloud and Townsend, *Boundaries,* 110.

28    *"God's ultimate goal for your life"*: Rick Warren, *The Purpose-Driven Life: What on Earth Am I Here For?* (Grand Rapids: Zondervan, 2002), 173.

*"If you want to become more like Jesus"*: Thomas, *Sacred Marriage,* 21.

## Chapter 3: You Don't Just Show Up and Go Up—A Step Back for Couples Still Dating

*page*

33    The epigraph to this chapter is drawn from Charles Houston, "Disorders Caused by Altitude," in *Medicine for Mountaineering & Other Wilderness Activities,* ed. James A. Wilkerson (Seattle: The Mountaineers Books, 2001), 228.

*"Taken abruptly from sea level"*: Wilkerson, *Medicine for Mountaineering,* 226.

34    *"At sea level...physical act of breathing"*: Robert Schoene, quoted in Broughton Coburn, *Everest: Mountain Without Mercy* (Washington, DC: National Geographic Society, 1997), 228.

*average breathing rate:* Tod Schimelpfenig and Linda Lindsey, *Wilderness First Aid* (Mechanicsburg, PA: Stackpole Books, 2000), 107.

35    *air pressure at various heights:* "The Killer Within," *National Geographic* (May 2003): 30–32.

*body reactions at nine thousand feet:* Schimelpfenig and Lindsey, *Wilderness First Aid,* 213–14.

*acute mountain sickness:* Schimelpfenig and Lindsey, *Wilderness First Aid,* 214.

36 *80 percent of the adaptations in first ten days:* Schimelpfenig and Lindsey, *Wilderness First Aid,* 213, 210.

37 *95 percent acclimatized by six weeks:* Schimelpfenig and Lindsey, *Wilderness First Aid,* 210.

*brain consumes 15 percent of the body's oxygen:* Michael Klesius, "The Body—Adjust or Die," *National Geographic* (May 2003): 33.

39 *"I realized that the attempt":* Ed Viesturs with Peter Potterfield, *Himalayan Quest* (Washington, DC: National Geographic Society, 2003), 35.

40 *"Climbing a mountain…getting down is mandatory":* Ed Viesturs (lecture, Recreational Equipment, Inc., Oakbrook, IL, October 17, 2003).

41 *"Dating efficiency is a function":* Neil Clark Warren, *How to Know If Someone Is Worth Pursuing in Two Dates or Less* (Nashville: Nelson, 1999), xii.

42–43 *"The payoff for all this self-discovery":* Warren, *How to Know,* 41.

43 *Must-Haves and Can't-Stands:* Warren, *How to Know,* 48.

44 *"For you created my inmost being":* Psalm 139:13–14.

45 *animal descriptors for personalities:* Gary Smalley and John Trent, *The Two Sides of Love: What Strengthens Affection, Closeness, and Lasting Commitment?* (Pomona, CA: Focus on the Family, 1990), 34–36.

*"Almost without exception":* Smalley and Trent, *The Two Sides of Love,* 30.

45–46 *when different personality types marry:* Florence Littauer and Marita Littauer, *Getting Along with Almost Anybody: The Complete Personality Book* (Grand Rapids: Revell, 1998), 336–39.

48 *"If you and your partner do not have the freedom":* Warren, *How to Know,* 71.

*highest elevation of permanent human habitation:* "The Killer Within," 31.

## Chapter 4: Up a Wall Without a Piton

*page*

51 The epigraph to this chapter is drawn from Daniel Duane, *El Capitan: Historic Feats and Radical Routes* (San Francisco: Chronicle Books, 2000), 39.

52 *"The exposure…preyed upon the stability"*: Duane, *El Capitan,* 19.

53 *"I was utterly and desperately terrified"*: Duane, *El Capitan,* 21.

*"single greatest adventure…with myself"*: Duane, *El Capitan,* 21.

54 *"He was one of those rare men"*: Duane, *El Capitan,* 23.

54–55 *discussion of Mescalito:* Duane, *El Capitan,* 23–27.

55 *"I had finally done the thing"*: Duane, *El Capitan,* 28.

57 *"Leading is a thinking person's game"*: Don Mellor, *Rock Climbing: A Trailside Guide* (New York: Norton, 1997), 112.

58 *"I've had hornets"*: Mellor, *Rock Climbing,* 132.

*"Much of the difficulty in breaking"*: Paul Piana, *Big Walls: Breakthroughs on the Free-Climbing Frontier* (San Francisco: Sierra Club, 1997), 28.

60 *"Manhood means moving"*: Lawrence J. Crabb, *God Calls Men to Move Beyond the Silence of Adam: Becoming Men of Courage in a World of Chaos* (Grand Rapids: Zondervan, 1995), 14.

65 *"Marriage cannot be successfully navigated"*: Henry Cloud and John Townsend, *Boundaries in Marriage* (Grand Rapids: Zondervan, 1999), 71.

66 *a man is made to fight:* John Eldredge, *Wild at Heart: Discovering the Secrets of a Man's Soul* (Nashville: Nelson, 2001), 140.

## Chapter 5: There's a Reason They Call It Terminal Velocity

*page*

69 The epigraph to this chapter is drawn from Jonathan Green, "You'll Be Cruising at an Altitude of 30,000 Feet," *Men's Journal* 12, no. 9 (October 2003): 96.

80   *"Commitment provides the time"*: Henry Cloud and John Townsend,
     *Boundaries in Marriage* (Grand Rapids: Zondervan, 1999), 120.


## Chapter 6: It's Not About the Bike, Really
*page*

87   The epigraph to this chapter is drawn from Ben Hewitt, "The
     Winning Gear," *Men's Journal* (October 2003): 63.

     *"I was built like a linebacker"*: Lance Armstrong with Sally Jenkins,
     *It's Not About the Bike: My Journey Back to Life* (New York: Putnam,
     2000), 66.

88   *"Measure the weight of the body"*: Lance Armstrong with Sally Jenkins,
     *Every Second Counts* (New York: Broadway Books, 2003), 168.

     *"If you weighed too little...power to weight"*: Armstrong with Jenkins,
     *Every Second Counts,* 157.

89   *"peaks that made riders crack"*: Armstrong with Jenkins, *It's Not About
     the Bike,* 238.

     *"You hunch over your handlebars"*: Armstrong with Jenkins, *It's Not
     About the Bike,* 240.

90   *"I surged again"*: Armstrong with Jenkins, *It's Not About the Bike,*
     241.

     *Armstrong's conversation with his coach:* Armstrong with Jenkins, *It's Not
     About the Bike,* 241–42.

91   *Friction among the bearings:* Frank Rowland Whitt and David Gordon
     Wilson, *Bicycling Science,* 2nd ed. (Cambridge, MA: MIT Press,
     1982), 145.

     *Joint friction:* Whitt and Wilson, *Bicycling Science,* 149.

92   *"Using an aero bar with elbow rests"*: Editors of *Bicycling* Magazine,
     *Bicycle Magazine's Ride Like a Pro* (Emmaus, PA: Rodale, 1992), 8.

93   *"Everyone who has ever lived"*: Henry Cloud, *Changes That Heal: How
     to Understand Your Past to Ensure a Healthier Future* (Grand Rapids:
     Zondervan, 1992), 208.

94 *"Our first task in life"*: David Stoop and James Masteller, *Forgiving Our Parents, Forgiving Ourselves: Healing Adult Children of Dysfunctional Families* (Ann Arbor, MI: Vine Books, 1991), 40–41.

96 *"Bonding is the ability"*: Cloud, *Changes That Heal,* 46.

97 *the difficulty of separating from others:* Cloud, *Changes That Heal,* 13.

*"In the simplest sense, a boundary"*: Henry Cloud and John Townsend, *Boundaries in Marriage* (Grand Rapids: Zondervan, 1999), 17.

98 *"Choices are the foundation"*: Cloud, *Changes That Heal,* 106.

99 *Armstrong is three minutes faster:* Armstrong with Jenkins, *Every Second Counts,* 156.

## Chapter 7: Up Where We Belong
### page

103 The epigraph to this chapter is drawn from Noel Whittall, *Paragliding: The Complete Guide* (New York: Lyons Press, 1995), 7.

107 *"The crux of cross-country flying"*: Will Gadd, "Thermals: Collectors, Wicks and Triggers," www.ushga.org.

108 *"At about 500 feet"*: "Flytec World Record Encampment."

109 *"Something very good or very bad"*: "Flytec World Record Encampment."

112–13 *"The usual myths"*: Robert T. Michael et al., *Sex in America: A Definitive Survey* (New York: Warner Books, 1994), 119–20.

113 *"Those having the most partnered sex"*: Michael et al., *Sex in America,* 131.

*average television viewer:* Robert Putnam, *Bowling Alone: The Collapse and Revival of American Community* (New York: Simon & Schuster, 2000), 222.

114 *death rate in divorced men:* Glenn T. Stanton, *Why Marriage Matters: Reasons to Believe in Marriage in Postmodern Society* (Colorado Springs: Piñon Press, 1997), 83.

*rate of alcoholism in divorced adults and suicide ratios:* Stanton, *Why Marriage Matters,* 77, 79.

*rates of major depression and mental illness:* Stanton, *Why Marriage Matters,* 86–87.

*"Being divorced and a non-smoker":* Stanton, *Why Marriage Matters,* 81.

115   *"Divorce carries multiple risks":* Barbara Dafoe Whitehead, *The Divorce Culture* (New York: Knopf, 1997), 93.

   *effect of divorce on children:* Judith Wallerstein, Julia Lewis, and Sandra Blakeslee, *The Unexpected Legacy of Divorce: The Landmark 25 Year Study* (New York: Hyperion, 2000), n.p.

116   *"Just as experience levels":* John Halle, "Luck, Longevity and the Limits of Skill," www.ushga.org.

117   *common marriage myths:* Les Parrott and Leslie Parrott, *Saving Your Marriage Before It Starts: Seven Questions to Ask Before (and After) You Marry* (Grand Rapids: Zondervan, 1995), 16–30.

## Chapter 8: The Trail Less Traveled

*page*
   121   The epigraph to this chapter is drawn from Dave King and Michael Kaminer, *The Mountain Bike Experience: A Complete Introduction to the Joys of Off-Road Riding* (New York: Henry Holt, 1996), 67.

   122   *"took the one less traveled":* Robert Frost, "The Road Not Taken," *The Poetry of Robert Frost,* ed. Edward Connery Lathem (New York: Holt, Rinehart and Winston, 1969), 105.

   123   *"Tense mountain bikers ride like ice cubes":* Ed Pavelka, ed., *Bicycle Magazine's Mountain Biking Skills: Tactics, Tips and Techniques to Master Any Terrain* (Emmaus, PA: Rodale, 2000), 11–12.

   124   *"the ones that keep your bike moving":* Bill Strickland, *Mountain Biking: The Ultimate Guide to the Ultimate Ride* (Camden, ME: Ragged Mountain Press, 1998), 30.

   125   *"the good line or no line":* Strickland, *Mountain Biking,* 30.

   *"A rotating front wheel":* Strickland, *Mountain Biking,* 73–74.

126   *"Your riding experience":* King and Kaminer, *The Mountain Bike Experience,* 5.

127   *five love languages:* Gary Chapman, *The Five Love Languages: How to Express Heartfelt Commitment to Your Mate* (Chicago: Northfield Publishing, 1995).

132   *"If your spouse's primary love language":* Chapman, *The Five Love Languages,* 109.

## Chapter 9: If It Were Easy, Everybody Would Be Doing It

page

137   The epigraph to this chapter is drawn from Matt Fitzgerald, *Triathlete Magazine's Complete Triathlon Book: The Training, Diet, Health, Equipment, and Safety Tips You Need to Do Your Best* (New York: Warner Books, 2003), xii.

141   *"Twenty miles of hope":* Joe Friel and Gordon Byrn, *Going Long: Training for Ironman-Distance Triathlons* (Boulder, CO: VeloPress, 2003), 163.

*"The race really begins":* Friel and Byrn, *Going Long,* 168.

*"If we cannot master…success as triathletes":* Fitzgerald, *Complete Triathlon Book,* 219.

142   *"Those with backgrounds in all three":* Sally Edwards with Rebecca Brocard Yao and Kaari Busick, *The Complete Book of Triathlons* (Roseville, CA: Prima Publishing, 2001), 258.

144   *"A couple's ability to deal with differences":* Henry Cloud and John Townsend, *Boundaries in Marriage* (Grand Rapids: Zondervan, 1999), 164.

*"Make conflict your ally":* Cloud and Townsend, *Boundaries in Marriage,* 165.

*hidden issues:* Howard Markman, Scott Stanley, and Susan L. Blumberg, *Fighting for Your Marriage: Positive Steps for Preventing Divorce and Preserving Lasting Love* (San Francisco: Jossey-Bass, 1994), 123–33.

145   *"feeling valued by your partner"*: Markman, Stanley, and Blumberg, *Fighting for Your Marriage,* 128.

*"the long-term security of the relationship"*: Markman, Stanley, and Blumberg, *Fighting for Your Marriage,* 129.

*"At the deepest level"*: Markman, Stanley, and Blumberg, *Fighting for Your Marriage,* 130.

146   *"If there is one similarity"*: John M. Gottman and Nan Silver, *The Seven Principles for Making Marriage Work* (New York: Crown, 1999), 159.

147   *"soft start-up"*: Gottman and Silver, *The Seven Principles,* 159.

147–48   *soft start-up advice:* Gottman and Silver, *The Seven Principles,* 164–65.

149   *four ways to escalate a discussion:* Markman, Stanley, and Blumberg, *Fighting for Your Marriage,* 13–20.

151   *69 percent of a couple's conflicts are perpetual:* Gottman and Silver, *The Seven Principles,* 130.

*"that which is innately different"*: Steve Bell and Valerie Bell, *Made to Be Loved: Enjoying Intimacy with God and Your Spouse* (Chicago: Moody, 1999), 110.

152   *"Left unaddressed, the rub can become"*: Bell and Bell, *Made to Be Loved,* 100.

*three-step process of "smoothing the rub"*: Bell and Bell, *Made to Be Loved,* 109–14.

154   *"Forgiveness is love's toughest work"*: Lewis B. Smedes, *Forgive and Forget: Healing the Hurts We Don't Deserve* (San Francisco: Harper & Row, 1984), xvi.

*"Forgiveness is a decision"*: Markman, Stanley, and Blumberg, *Fighting for Your Marriage,* 217.

*"Forgiveness as a process"*: David Stoop and James Masteller, *Forgiving Our Parents, Forgiving Ourselves: Healing Adult Children of Dysfunctional Families* (Ann Arbor, MI: Vine Books, 1991), 211.

156–57 *"I have discovered this one incontrovertible truth"*: Eric Harr, *Triathlon Training in Four Hours a Week: From Beginner to Finish Line in Just Six Weeks* (Emmaus, PA: Rodale, 2003), 216.

## Chapter 10: Catch a Wave, and You're Sitting on Top of the World
page

159 The epigraph to this chapter is drawn from Peter Dixon, *The Complete Guide to Surfing* (Guilford, CT: Lyons Press, 2001), xv.

160 *"The longer the wavelength"*: Dixon, *The Complete Guide to Surfing*, 54.

   *swells moving through the ocean:* Matt Warshaw, *The Encyclopedia of Surfing* (Orlando: Harcourt, 2003), 685.

161 *less than a hundred big-wave surfers:* Jon Krakauer, "Mark Foo's Last Ride," *Outside* 20, no. 5 (May 1995), http://www.outside.away .com/outside/magazine, 3.

162 *twenty days of surfing a year:* Matt Warshaw, *Maverick's: The Story of Big Wave Surfing* (San Francisco: Chronicle Books, 2003), 42.

   *length of a Maverick's ride:* Warshaw, *The Encyclopedia of Surfing*, 370.

   *"It's created junkies...we always will":* Ken Bradshaw, quoted in Warshaw, *Maverick's*, xiii.

163 *"The bottom configuration...happen next":* Krakauer, "Mark Foo's Last Ride," 11.

   *"If you want to ride the ultimate wave":* Krakauer, "Mark Foo's Last Ride," 4.

165 *"so thick and powerful":* Drew Kampion, *Stoked!: A History of Surf Culture* (Salt Lake City: Gibbs Smith, 2003), 187.

   *"The wave just [fell] away":* Daniel Duane, "Last Man Standing," *Men's Journal* (July 2004): 70.

   *"single solid lip":* Duane, "Last Man Standing," 70.

   *"driven through a cheese grater":* Duane, "Last Man Standing," 70.

166  *"If you want to try this":* Sam George, ed., *The Perfect Day: 40 Years of Surfer Magazine* (San Francisco: Chronicle Press, 2001), 141.

167–68  *"The essence of sexual intimacy":* Tim Alan Gardner, *Sacred Sex: A Spiritual Celebration of Oneness in Marriage* (Colorado Springs: WaterBrook, 2002), 48.

172–73  *advice to husbands and wives from Amy and Tim Gardner:* Gardner, *Sacred Sex,* 113–14.

176  *"If you want to ride":* Krakauer, "Mark Foo's Last Ride," 4.

177  *"Being sexually intimate":* Gardner, *Sacred Sex,* 125.

## Chapter 11: Rapids, as in Fast Moving

*page*

179  The epigraph to this chapter is drawn from Gordon Grant, "Patterns of Grace for Moments of Stress," in *Whitewater Kayaking,* ed. Dave Harrison (Harrisburg, PA: Stackpole Books, 1998), 56.

180  *"You have to be 'spot on'":* Stephen B. U'Ren, *Performance Kayaking* (Harrisburg, PA: Stackpole Books, 1990), 86.

184  *"Few other sports require the processing":* Peter Heller, "Liquid Thunder," *Outside* (July 2002): 88.

188  *change as a shift in external circumstances:* William Bridges, *Managing Transitions: Making the Most of Change* (Cambridge, MA: Perseus Publishing, 1991), 3.

190  *change followed by a neutral zone:* Bridges, *Managing Transitions,* 6.

191  *"Every transition begins…the new":* William Bridges, *Transitions: Making Sense of Life's Changes* (Cambridge, MA: Perseus Publishing, 1980), 11.

## Chapter 12: Reaching the Void

*page*

195  The epigraph to this chapter is drawn from Joe Simpson, *Touching the Void* (New York: Harper & Row, 1988), 107.

*"We climbed because it was fun...then it wasn't"*: *Touching the Void,* directed by Kevin Macdonald (2004: IFC Films).

196    *"Four days...Five at the outside"*: Simpson, *Touching the Void,* 22.

197    *"It looks hairy"*: Simpson, *Touching the Void,* 46.

198    *"You're dead"*: Simpson, *Touching the Void,* 67.

203    *"The change in me was astonishing"*: Simpson, *Touching the Void,* 113.

205–6    *"It was impossible to judge"*: Simpson, *Touching the Void,* 134.

208    *"It felt so normal to hurt"*: Simpson, *Touching the Void,* 151.

209    *"The night remained black"*: Simpson, *Touching the Void,* 158.

*"Joe! Is that you?"*: Simpson, *Touching the Void,* 159.

212    *"Reassessment is the prevailing theme"*: Jim Conway, *Men in Midlife Crisis,* rev. ed. (Colorado Springs: Victor Books, 1997), 33.

## Chapter 13: They Told You About the Guano, Right?

page

219    The epigraph to this chapter is drawn from Michael Ray Taylor, *Caves: Exploring Hidden Realms* (Washington, DC: National Geographic Society, 2000), 10.

221    *"emotion of alarm"*: *American-Heritage Dictionary,* 2nd college edition, s.v. "fear."

223–26    *Fred Hutchison story:* Michael Ray Taylor, "Going Deep: How a Curmudgeonly Caver Discovered a Subterranean Wonder, Infuriated an Entire Sport and Then Rescued the Cavern from Ruin," *Sports Illustrated* 98, no. 9, March 3, 2003, 62–68.

225    *"The best way to begin"*: Taylor, *Caves: Exploring Hidden Realms,* 166.

*"the size of an office wastebasket"*: Taylor, "Going Deep," 64.

*"a vast expanse of blackness"*: Taylor, "Going Deep," 65.

*"Smith tossed a rock...enormous chamber"*: Taylor, "Going Deep," 65.